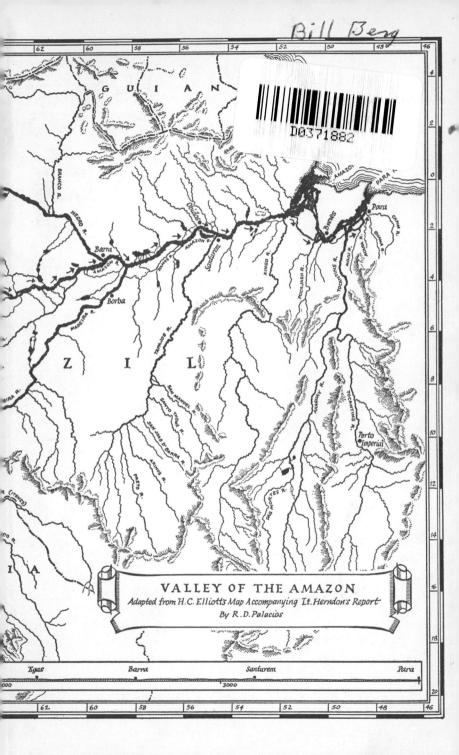

VALLEY OF THE AMAZON

Adapted from H.C. Elliott's Map Accompanying Lt. Herndon's Report

By R.D. Palacios

Exploration of the
Valley of the Amazon

GREAT ADVENTURE LIBRARY

By WILLIAM LEWIS HERNDON

Exploration of the Valley of the Amazon

EDITED AND WITH AN INTRODUCTION BY

HAMILTON BASSO

ILLUSTRATED WITH MAPS AND REPRODUCTIONS
OF CONTEMPORARY PRINTS

NEW YORK GROSSET & DUNLAP PUBLISHERS

CONTENTS

LIST OF ILLUSTRATIONS

INTRODUCTION

William Lewis Herndon and His Book

*   *   *

It is curious that a book of such great merit as William Lewis Herndon's *Exploration of the Valley of the Amazon* should have been forgotten for so long a time. Published in 1854, it has never been reprinted. In its own day, however, it could hardly have aroused more interest. Mark Twain, reading its pages as a young man of twenty-one, was so carried away that he determined to seek his fortune in South America. It was this ambition that caused him to go down the Mississippi to New Orleans for the first time (traveling on a steamboat which happened to be piloted by a man named Horace Bixby) and that subsequently led him to describe Herndon's book as one of the major turning points of his life. Other readers found the volume no less absorbing, if not quite so influential. It was received with as much enthusiasm as Charles Wilkes's *Narrative,* the report of his Pacific and Antarctic explorations, which appeared in 1844, and the various travel books of John Lloyd Stephens, the most important of which, *Incidents of Travel in Central America, Chiapas, and Yucatan,* was published in 1841.

Wilkes was a much more consequential figure in the

ix

realm of exploration than either Herndon or Stephens. Like Christopher Columbus, it fell to him to come across a new world—the vast Antarctic continent which he sighted west of the Balleny Islands in December, 1839, and part of which, known as Wilkes Land, still bears his name. But if Herndon and Stephens discovered no new worlds, they may be said to have rediscovered old ones. Each called the attention of his time to distant, historic lands that had all but dropped from sight. Stephens awakened an interest in Central America and Mexico that has persisted ever since, and Herndon, as Van Wyck Brooks has noted,* caused almost as much excitement by his pioneer "opening" of South America as Commodore Perry by his actual opening of Japan.

Were that Herndon's only accomplishment, however, there would be no justification for this new edition of his book. Its claim to our notice lies in its being one of the best pieces of travel writing in our literature. I have no wish to dispute the assertion, first made by Brooks and then by others, that John Lloyd Stephens was the greatest of American travel writers. Let us agree that he is. It seems to me, though, that in this book Herndon comes close to challenging Stephens on his own ground. If its literary excellence has been overlooked, it is because Herndon has been overlooked. Furthermore, appearing originally as a government report,† the book was full of lists, timetables, boiling points, meteorological observations, and other impedimenta that, while necessary at the time, got in the way of its narrative flow. Herndon, admit-

* Van Wyck Brooks, *The Times of Melville and Whitman,* p. 195. E. P. Dutton & Co., Inc., New York, 1947.

† House of Representatives Executive Document 53, Thirty-third Congress, First Session (Washington, 1854).

tedly, does not "write" as well as Stephens; we miss the latter's grace and skill. But Herndon's straightforward, manly, vigorous style is hardly less effective for not striving after effect, and if he does not go in for literary display, his book displays several of the qualities that make for literature.

It might be well here to assemble some of the facts of Herndon's life and to explain how, nine years before the Civil War, he became the first American to descend the Amazon from its upper tributaries in Peru to its mouth, nearly 4,000 miles away, in the Atlantic Ocean. Even if we had no other information about Herndon, we would know from his book that he was a Virginian. Atop a Peruvian mountain called Puy-puy, 15,000 feet above sea level, the snipes, ducks, and other aquatic birds that he was astonished to find at so high an altitude reminded him of the duck shooting in the marches of the Rappahannock. Talking with a Scotchman named McCulloch, who was trying to establish a sugar plantation on the banks of the Rio Negro (one of the tributaries of the Amazon), he advised him to set fire to his fields after every cutting, a common practice in the Virginia tobacco country at the time. And over and over again, as if of its own accord, his Southern romanticism must find a way out. Reporting to his government on the location, water, population, and general appearance of one of the villages at which he chanced to stop, he added: "I noticed, also, a tree bearing a large bell-shaped flower called *floripondo*. This is an old acquaintance of mine. It gives out a delicious fragrance at night, which accompanied, as I have known it, by soft air, rich moonlight, and gentle company makes bare existence a happiness." In another place, after mentioning one of the many snowstorms that overtook him while crossing the Andes, he noted: "About fifteen miles from Junin we passed the village of Carhuamayo. Here I saw the only really pretty face I have met within the Sierra and bought a glass of pisco from it." *

Herndon, at the time of the *floripondo* and the only really pretty face he met within the Sierra, was thirty-eight years old. His father, Dabney Herndon, was a descendant of William Herndon, who came to America in 1674, and his mother, Elizabeth Hull, was a member of a long-established Virginia family. One of seven children, William Lewis was orphaned when a boy. Entering the United States Navy as a midshipman in 1828, when he was fifteen, he received his lieutenant's commission in 1841, when he was twenty-eight. His first duty was seen aboard the frigate *Guerrière,* on which he served for three years, mostly in the Pacific. He was then assigned to the *Constellation,* spending upwards of two years in the Mediterranean, and in 1834 was ordered aboard the *Independence,* which cruised the coastal waters of South America for more than a year. In 1836, returning to the United States, Herndon married Frances Elizabeth Hansbrough. Their daughter Ellen later became the wife of Chester A. Arthur, the twentieth President of the United States.

In 1843, now a lieutenant, Herndon was assigned to the Depot of Charts and Instruments in Washington. The Depot, which in time became the United States Naval Observatory and Hydrographic Office, was headed by Lieut.

---

* There is, of course, no reason to imagine that a New Englander would have been any less susceptible to these various South American charms; what is hard to imagine is his writing them into a government report.

(afterwards Commander) Matthew Fontaine Maury. Although only thirty-seven years old at the time, Maury had already laid the basis for his reputation as one of the fathers of modern oceanography. His *A New Theoretical and Practical Treatise on Navigation* had been published in 1836, when he was but thirty, and he was also known for a series of articles on naval reform and other subjects which, under the title of "Our Navy; Scraps from the Lucky Bag," had appeared in *The Southern Literary Messenger*.

Maury and Herndon were cousins, and Maury, in 1834, had married one of Herndon's sisters. Despite this dual connection, the young superintendent was not inclined to spare his new assistant. Himself a man of prodigious industry, holding to the theory that the only talent worth having was a talent for hard work, Maury kept Herndon busy far into the night making astronomical calculations which he used in connection with the exhaustive study he was making of winds and currents. Out of Maury's labors came his famous "Winds and Currents Chart," one of the revolutionary documents of modern navigation; out of Herndon's came a nervous breakdown that forced him to resign from the Observatory after three years.

Meanwhile, in 1846, the Mexican War had broken out. Herndon was given command of a small steamer, the *Isis,* which operated more or less uneventfully in the Gulf of Mexico for eighteen months. At the conclusion of hostilities, apparently restored in health, he returned to the Observatory and Maury's severe employment for another year. He was then again assigned to foreign duty, this time aboard the *Vandalia* of the Pacific squadron, and it was in August, 1850, while he was aboard the *Vandalia*, en route to the Sandwich Islands and lying at anchor in the harbor of Valparaiso, Chile, that he received notice that he had been ordered to explore the Amazon valley.

Taking leave of the *Vandalia,* Herndon went from Chile to Peru. He was joined in Lima by twenty-year-old Passed Midshipman (later Lieut.) Lardner Gibbon, who handed him his official orders. A native of Philadelphia, Gibbon, like Herndon, had joined the Navy when he was fifteen. The expedition's second-in-command, he had some talent as an artist and draughtsman. He accompanied Herndon across the Andes, sketching as he went, and his finished drawings, four of which are reproduced in this volume, were lithographed as illustrations for Herndon's book.

Having negotiated the Andes and reached the Peruvian tributaries of the Amazon, Herndon and Gibbon parted company—Herndon to make the voyage described in his narrative, and Gibbon to cross over into Bolivia and begin his own descent of the Amazon by embarking upon the headwaters of one of its Bolivian tributaries. The two men were not to see each other again until they met in Washington almost two years later. Gibbon wrote an account of his adventures, which was published in 1854 as the second volume of *Exploration of the Valley of the Amazon.* It has a kind of earnest, simple naïveté that gives it a certain boyish charm, but for the most part it is so pedestrian and poorly written that only the most confirmed addicts of travel writing are likely to find it of any interest.

Herndon's assignment, unusual though it may seem today, was part of the texture of the times. The United

States was then in the midst of an age of discovery and exploration that was hardly less impressive than the similar ages of England and Spain. Beginning with the expedition of Lewis and Clark in 1804, it reached its climax in 1854, when, by the treaty of Kanagawa, Com. Matthew Calbraith Perry finally brought about the opening up of Japan. In addition to Wilkes's voyage to the Pacific islands and the Antarctic, Lieut. John P. Gillis had headed an astronomical expedition to Chile, Lieut. William Francis Lynch had been dispatched to explore the Red Sea, and Lieut. Archibald McRae had traversed the pampas from Chile to Buenos Aires. In the 1850s, Comdr. Candwalder Ringgold and later Comdr. John Rodgers were sent to "explore and survey" the Bering Strait, the North Pacific, and the China Sea; Lieut. Isaac G. Strain went on a similar mission to the Isthmus of Darien; and Lieut. Richard L. Page was instructed to investigate the Rio de la Plata and its tributaries.

During the period 1804–1854, a considerable amount of exploring also went on at home. The acquisition of Louisiana and the Lewis and Clark Expedition initiated an era of curiosity about the western United States that had its first reflection in Lieut. Zebulon N. Pike's exploration of the upper reaches of the Mississippi in 1805–1806, followed by his more famous expedition to the Southwest in 1806–1807. After Pike, in 1819–1820, came Maj. Stephen H. Long's exploration of the Platte, the Arkansas, and the Red rivers, and in 1823 his voyage up the St. Peter's River in Minnesota to explore the country, locate the 49th degree of latitude, and take possession of all the territory below it. Two years later, in 1825, an expedition commanded by Gen. Henry Atchison made its way to the

Yellowstone River, and in 1842 John C. Frémont led the first of his three official expeditions to the Far West and California.

Herndon's mission, though part of a general pattern, must not be regarded as having been prompted by mere geographical curiosity on the part of the United States. His orders were detailed, explicit, and to the point. "The government desires to be put in possession of certain information relating to the valley of the river Amazon. . . . This desire extends not only to the present condition of the valley, with regard to the navigability of its streams, but also to its capacities for cultivation and to the character and extent of its undeveloped commercial resources, whether of the field, the forest, the river, or the mine. . . . You will make such geographical and scientific observations by the way as may be consistent with the main object of the expedition, always bearing in mind that these are merely incidental, and that no part of the main objects of the expedition is to be interfered with by them."

But why, in February, 1851, the desire for this particular kind of information? A large part of the answer, though not the whole of it, is contained in the fact that only six months earlier, in September, 1850, Dom Pedro II, the Emperor of Brazil, had approved a law authorizing steam navigation on the Amazon. Already, in Rio de Janeiro, the *Compania de Navegação e Commèrcio do Amazonas* was in the process of being organized, and, in London, the English were wondering if trade might again follow the flag. Actually, their curiosity on that score antedated that of Washington by a good fifteen years. Lieut. William Smith of the Royal Navy had been sent in 1835 on a journey from Lima to Pará, "undertaken with a view of ascertaining the practicability of a navigable communication with the Atlantic," and had published a book about it.* Since Herndon mentions the volume several times in his text, we may be sure it had been read in Washington, especially by Matthew Fontaine Maury. For despite his absorbing interest in winds, currents, and other aspects of oceanography, Maury was hardly less interested in the opening up of the Amazon to free trade in general and American trade in particular.

Although there is no evidence to indicate that Maury was directly responsible for Herndon's mission, we may be reasonably certain that he had a large hand in it. The opening of the Amazon Valley to steam navigation, beneficial though it might prove to be to the American economy, had for Maury an even higher value. He saw it as a means of preserving the Union. As a Virginian, Maury was naturally sympathetic to the hopes and ambitions of the South, but even as a Virginian he was not completely blinded by sectional loyalties. Recognizing the explosive potentialities of slavery, he had gradually evolved his own remedy for getting rid of it—let the slaves of the South be sold to the planters of the Amazon and then prohibit slavery in the South by law.

"The Southern states," he wrote in 1850, "may *emancipate* just as New York and Massachusetts. But large numbers of slaves were not set free. They, after the emancipation acts became laws, were sold to the South, and so the South may sell to the Amazon. The slaves of the South are worth 15 hundred million. Their value is

* W. Smith and F. Lowe, *Narrative of a Journey from Lima to Pará, by the Rivers Pachitea, Ucayali, and Amazon.* London, 1836.

increasing at the rate of 30 or 40 million a year. It is the industrial capital of the South. Did ever a people consent to sink so much industrial capital by emancipation or any other voluntary act?'' *

It seems hardly necessary to say that Herndon was not sent to explore the Amazon with the purpose of furthering Maury's scheme. His instructions came from the Navy, not from his brother-in-law, and the Navy was interested in what it said it was interested in—trade, commerce, natural resources—and not in how to rid the South of slaves. Nowhere in Herndon's orders is the Southern slave question mentioned and nowhere in his book does he touch on it as such. There is one place, however, where, again the Southerner, he betrays his concern over the deepening rift between the North and South. Describing his arrival in Barra, one of the larger Brazilian communities of the time, he tells how he was extended the hospitality of an Italian merchant, Senhor Enrique Antonii, in whose house he became a guest. After remarking upon his snug, comfortable quarters, he goes on to say: ''The greatest treat that I met here, however, was a file of New York papers. They were not very recent it is true, but still six months more recent than anything I have seen from home, and I read them with great interest and no small anxiety.''

What Herndon thought of Maury's scheme for ridding the South of slavery we do not know. That they discussed it together would appear to be inevitable, and it is almost certain that Herndon, upon his return to the United States, gave Maury certain information that was not contained

* Charles Lee Lewis, *Matthew Fontaine Maury, Pathfinder of the Seas,* p. 118. U.S. Naval Institute, Annapolis, 1927.

in his report. In any event, Maury used Herndon's findings to press his argument for the opening of the Amazon to free navigation. Herndon's report was submitted to Congress on January 26, 1853. Shortly thereafter, in the Washington *National Intelligencer & Union,* there appeared a series of articles written by Maury and signed "Inca," in which the commercial, mineral, and agricultural possibilities of the Amazon Valley were highly—at times too highly—praised. The free navigation of the river was demanded by Maury in the Inca articles. He brought the same demand formally to the attention of Congress in "A Memorial by Lieutenant Maury in Behalf of the Free Navigation of the Amazon," and the Inca articles became the basis for his most popular book, *Letters on the Amazon and Atlantic Slopes of South America.*

It was not until fourteen years after Herndon returned from South America that Brazil, which controlled the vast lower stretches of the Amazon and its all-important mouth at Pará, finally consented, in July, 1867, to the opening of the river to vessels of all flags. By then, however, it was too late to do Maury or his plan for the eradication of slavery much good. Having followed Virginia out of the Union and been ruined by the Civil War, the aging oceanographer was then in exile in England. But no one man played a larger part in the opening of the Amazon to free navigation than Maury, and it is time that Herndon be given credit for his contribution to the enterprise.*

* Having been drawn this far into Maury's story, it may be well to fill in the rest of it. After the Civil War he went to Mexico where he became Imperial Commissioner of Emigration to Emperor Maximilian, at whose invitation he attempted to establish a colony of Virginian émigrés. Maximilian eventually abandoned his scheme, though not before the colonists

Herndon, though less fortunate than Maury, was spared his painful choice and his years of troubled exile. Raised to the rank of commander in 1855, he was granted a leave of absence by the Navy to take command of the mail steamer *George Law* of the Pacific Line. The vessel, re-christened the *Central American* a few months after Herndon assumed command, ran between New York and Colón. It carried both passengers and freight. All ships of the Pacific Line, which had a government subsidy, were commanded by officers of the United States Navy. Herndon, after two routine years as master of the *Central American,* ran into a heavy gale off Cape Hatteras on the morning of September 11, 1857. Aboard his vessel was a cargo of gold from California, a large accumulation of mail, and 575 passengers. By midmorning the gale mounted to the proportions of a full-fledged storm. Part of the rigging of the *Central American* was carried away, and it sprang a leak in the forward part of its hull. Such a mass of water poured into the steamer that its boilers were extinguished. Herndon, left with a dead ship that wallowed in every wave and was sure to founder, appealed for help by sending up flares. The signals were answered by the brig *Marine,* to which all the women and children aboard the *Central American* were transferred before the onset of night and the furiously raging seas ended the work of rescue. The *Central American* went down with 232 per-

---

had introduced the cultivation of cinchona to Mexico, and in 1866 Maury took ship for England. There he was presented with a fund raised by public subscription, and among various other honors was awarded the LL.D. by Cambridge University. In 1868, after a general amnesty permitted his return to America, he became professor of meteorology in the Virginia Military Institute, and settled in Lexington, Virginia, where he died on February 1, 1873.

sons, Herndon among them. A monument to his memory stands on the grounds of the Naval Academy at Annapolis.

The appeal of all travel writing is that it tells the story of a journey. If the element of danger is present, as in the 4,000-mile journey of Capt. William Bligh in an open boat, and the adventures of Mungo Park in the interior of Africa, it naturally makes for a better story. But even when there is no danger, and nothing more hazardous is involved than the bouncing of a burro or the spurts of tobacco juice aimed carelessly by ill-mannered Americans, as in Robert Louis Stevenson's *Travels with a Donkey* and Harriet Martineau's *Retrospect of Western Travel,* the mere description of a journey and the scenes and incidents observed along the way is enough to engage the reader's interest and carry him along.

Herndon's narrative belongs in the latter category. He had to put up with hardships, difficulties, and an infinite number of minor exasperations, but at no time was he faced with any real threat of peril or disaster. Had he wanted to, however, he might have given that impression. One of the various merits of his book is the merit of understatement. He makes traveling down the Amazon seem hardly more hazardous than traveling down the Hudson. Sometimes, as when he finally reached the mainstream of the river after months of travel and realized that he still had many more months to go, he permitted himself the luxury of discouragement—but only rarely.

In the hands of a person of less sensibility, Herndon's narrative might have resulted, at best, in a work of competent journalism. Part of the journalist's responsibility was imposed on him by the nature of his mission, and he assumed it as a matter of course; but the values that journalism tends to emphasize, stressing the extraordinary, the shocking, and the bizarre, apparently had no interest or appeal for him.

The dance [of certain Indians] was a simple affair so far as figure was concerned—the women whirling round in the center, and the men (who were also the musicians) trotting around them in a circle. The music was made by rude drums, and fifes of reed, and it was quite amusing to see the alcalde, a large, painted, grave-looking Indian, trotting round like a dog on a treadmill, with a penny whistle in his mouth.

—

Two of our turtles died yesterday, and the Indians are eating them today. Ijurra suspects that they killed them, but Ijurra is of a suspicious nature, especially where Indians are concerned. We found the current today to be two miles per hour. A fish about two feet long, and sharp-built like a dolphin, jumped into the boat. It had two curved and very sharp teeth, like those of a squirrel, or the fangs of a serpent, in the lower jaw. It made us a very good mess.

—

At night we had a ball at the governor's house. The alcalde, who was a trump, produced his fiddle. Another had a rude sort of guitar, or banjo. Under the excitement of the music we danced until eleven o'clock. The Señor Commandante was in considerable request, and a fat old lady, who would not dance with anybody else, neary killed me.

—

Went to church. The congregation—men, women, and children—numbered about fifty. The service was conducted by the governor, assisted by the alcalde. A little, naked, bow-legged Indian child of two or three years, and Ijurra's pointer puppy, which he had brought all the way from Lima on his saddle-bow, worried the congregation with their tricks and gambols; but altogether they were attentive to their prayers, and devout. I enjoyed exceedingly the public worship of God with these simple people of the forest; and, although they probably understood little of what they were about, I thought I could see its humanizing and fraternizing effect upon all.

Here is Herndon at his consistent average. He betters these passages any number of times, but on the whole his book is made up of just such little pictures as these—clear, sharp, exact. He brought to his task an eye for significant detail, a boundless curiosity, a large sympathy for all kinds and conditions of people, the informed interest of a natural naturalist, a most engaging kind of humor, and what can only be described as a sense of fun. It is this appreciation of fun—the fun he obviously had with the fat old lady who almost danced him to death, for instance— that makes him such a pleasant companion and which, along with his humor, gives his narrative its special, individual tone. One wonders what else could be asked of a man, and, far harder to understand, why his book has gone neglected for nearly a hundred years. Our literature is not so rich in travel writing that we can afford to be so careless.

Aside from its literary quality, Herndon's book has a further interest attached to the influence it had upon Mark Twain—enough influence to cause Mark to call it, as has already been noted, one of the turning points of his life. The time was 1856; the place, Keokuk, Iowa. Then twenty-one years old, Mark was working for his older brother, Orion, who had moved to Keokuk and set himself up as a job printer. Mark was getting five dollars a week and board. His relations with Orion, as usual, were not always of the best. In a letter to his mother written from Keokuk on June 10, 1856, he aired his general dissatisfaction— he was being asked to do too many things at once; his help had been taken away from him; he was forced to work without plan or system; and, as a direct consequence of the helter-skelter nature of Orion's shop, he had failed to turn out a job on schedule for the first time.*

But the source of his dissatisfaction he failed to mention. The truth of the matter was that he had a bad case of South American fever. He had read Herndon's book and wanted to get to the headwaters of the Amazon. A little more than two months after his letter of June 10, he wrote to another brother, Henry, saying that it was his intention to start for Brazil, if possible, in six weeks. "I shall take care," he added, "that Ma and Orion are plentifully supplied with South American books. They have Herndon's report now." †

Then, as today, it took a certain amount of money to go adventuring, and Keokuk, Iowa, was a long way from the Amazon. However, Mark's mind was made up. He saved what he could out of his five dollars a week, and then, on a cold, bleak, gray day in early November—but why presume to tell a story that he has told himself?

Among the books that interested me in those days (he wrote in his article, "The Turning Point of My Life" ‡) was one about the Amazon. The traveller told an alluring tale of his long voyage up

* Albert Bigelow Paine, *Mark Twain: A Biography*, Centennial Edition, p. 108. Harper & Brothers, New York, 1936.

† Albert Bigelow Paine, ed., *Mark Twain's Letters*, p. 35. Harper & Brothers, New York, 1917.

‡ From *What Is Man and Other Essays*, Harper & Brothers, New York, 1906.

the great river from Pará to the sources of the Madeira,* through the heart of an enchanted land, a land wastefully rich in tropical wonders, a romantic land where all the birds and flowers and animals were of the museum varieties, and where the alligator and the crocodile and the monkey seemed as much at home as if they were in the Zoo. Also, he told an astonishing tale about *coca,* a vegetable product of miraculous powers: asserting that it was so nourishing and so strength-giving that the native of the mountains of the Madeira region would tramp up hill and down all day on a pinch of powdered coca and require no other sustenance.

I was fired with a longing to ascend the Amazon. Also with a longing to open up a trade in coca with all the world. During months I dreamed that dream, and tried to contrive ways to get to Pará and spring that splendid enterprise upon an unsuspecting planet. But all in vain. A person may *plan* as much as he wants to, but nothing of consequence is likely to come of it until the magician *Circumstance* steps in and takes the matter off his hands. At last Circumstance came to my help. It was in this way. Circumstance, to help or hurt another man, made him lose a fifty-dollar bill in the street; and to help or hurt me, made me find it. I advertised the find, and left for the Amazon the same day.

Then, after pointing out that circumstance, powerful though it may be, cannot work alone and must have a partner—a man's temperament—Mark continued:

A Circumstance that will coerce one man will have no effect upon a man of a different temperament. If Circumstance had thrown the banknote in Caesar's way, his temperament would not have made him start for the Amazon. His temperament would have compelled him to do something with the money, but not that. It might have made him advertise the note—and *wait*. We can't tell. Also, it might have made him go to New York and buy into the govern-

* Mark's memory, as sometimes happened, was at fault. Herndon went down the river, not up.

ment; with results that would leave Tweed nothing to learn when it came his turn.

Very well, Circumstance furnished the capital, and my temperament told me what to do with it. Sometimes a temperament is an ass. When that is the case the owner of it is an ass, too, and is going to remain one. Training, experience, association can temporarily so polish him, improve him, exalt him that people will think he is a mule, but they will be mistaken. Artificially he *is* a mule, for the time being, but at bottom he is an ass yet, and will remain one.

By temperament I was the kind of person that *does* things. Does them, and reflects afterward. So I started for the Amazon, without reflecting, and without asking any questions. That was more than fifty years ago. In all that time my temperament has not changed, by even a shade. I have been punished many and many a time, and bitterly, for doing things and reflecting afterward, but these tortures have been of no value to me: I still do the thing commanded by Circumstance and Temperament, and reflect afterward. Always violently. When I am reflecting, on those occasions, even deaf persons can hear me think. I went by the way of Cincinnati, and down the Ohio and Mississippi. My idea was to take ship, at New Orleans, for Pará. In New Orleans I inquired and found there was no ship leaving for Pará. Also, that there never had *been* one leaving for Pará. I reflected. A policeman came and asked me what I was doing, and I told him. He made me move on, and said if he caught me reflecting in the public street again he would run me in.

After a few days I was out of money. Then Circumstance arrived, with another turning-point of my life—a new link. On my way down, I had made the acquaintance of a pilot. I begged him to teach me the river, and he consented. I became a pilot.

With *Life on the Mississippi* and *Huckleberry Finn* in mind, it is difficult to believe that Mark Twain would not have become a pilot, regardless of Circumstance, young dreams of adventure, and wind-blown fifty-dollar bills. But there is his story of how it happened, and his judgment of the part that Herndon played in the development of his career.

One wonders, however, if the influence of Herndon's book might not have been greater than even he understood, and, in particular, if it may not have been one of the inspirations of *Life on the Mississippi*. To say that Mark Twain got the scheme of his book from Herndon's —both being made up in large part of the scenes and incidents of river life and people and adventures encountered along the way—would be saying too much. We know, however, that when Mark Twain wrote his "Turning Point" article in 1910, more than half a century after he read Herndon's narrative, it was still one of his most vivid recollections. Is it too far-fetched, then, to suspect that it was no less vivid when he sat down to write *Life on the Mississippi,* and that the general drift of his book may have been influenced, at least to some degree, by the almost identical pattern of *Exploration of the Valley of the Amazon?* I think not.

In preparing this edition of *Exploration of the Valley of the Amazon* I have done little more than strike out the mass of data that, because of the nature of his mission, Herndon had to include. In addition, I have made some alterations in the narrative itself, again for the most part striking out material that seemed to me to have little contemporary interest (such as a description of the way sugar cane was grown on a South American hacienda in 1852), and I have also made various changes in spelling and punctuation. Nothing has been done, however, to alter the intent or spirit of the original text, and my principal objective, throughout, has been to let Herndon speak for himself.

The maps reproduced in this book were drawn from maps of the period. In general, where there was a difference between the original map and the text, the cartographer has followed the usage of the text. When a place name on the map did not appear in the text, he has followed the usage of the original maps. All footnotes to the text, unless identified by my initials, are by Herndon.

That I am happy to have this chance to bring Herndon to the attention of a modern audience goes without saying. I wish, however, to express my thanks to Edward C. Aswell and Curtis G. Benjamin, both of McGraw-Hill Book Company, Inc., each of whom generously agreed with me that a new edition of his work was long overdue.

HAMILTON BASSO

WESTON, CONNECTICUT
August 20, 1951

Exploration of the
Valley of the Amazon

CHAPTER I

* * *

Attached to the U.S. ship *Vandalia,* of the Pacific squadron, lying at anchor in the harbor of Valparaiso, in the month of August, 1850, I received a communication from the Superintendent of the National Observatory informing me that orders to explore the Valley of the Amazon would be sent me by the next mail steamer.

The *Vandalia* was then bound for the Sandwich Islands, but Captain Gardner, with that kindness which ever characterized his intercourse with his officers, did not hesitate to detach me from the ship, and to give me permission to await, at Valparaiso, the arrival of my instructions.

Owing to the death of President Taylor and the consequent change in the Cabinet, my orders were delayed, and I spent several weeks in Valparaiso, and Santiago, the capital of Chile. This time, however, was not thrown away. My residence in these cities improved my knowledge of the Spanish language, and gave me information regarding the Bolivian tributaries of the Amazon which I probably could have got nowhere else.

After I had obtained from my Santiago and Valparaiso friends all the information that they would give me, I determined to proceed to Lima, Peru, and accordingly embarked on board the mail boat of the 26th of January.

1

My residence in Valparaiso had made new friends and established new ties that I found painful to break, but this is the lot of the navy officer. Separated from his family for years, he is brought into the closest and most intimate association with his messmates, and forms ties which are made but to be broken, generally by many years of separation. Taken from these, he is thrown among strangers, and becomes dependent upon their kindness and hospitality for the only enjoyments that make his life endurable.

I arrived in Lima on the 6th of February, 1851. This city had changed greatly since I was there, twenty years ago. Though we had bull-fights on the accession of the new President (which accession, strange to say, took place without popular tumult, except a small outbreak at Arequipa, resulting in the immediate imprisonment at Lima of the opposing candidate), yet the noble amphitheatre was not crowded as in old times with the *élite* and fashion of Lima. The ladies have given up their peculiar and most graceful national costume, the *Saya y Manto*, and it is now the mark of a ragged reputation. They dress in the French style, frequent the opera, and instead of the *Yerba de Paraguay*,* called Matté, of which they used a great quantity formerly, they now take tea.

My first business at Lima was to establish relations with Don Francisco Paula y Vigil, the accomplished and learned superintendent of the public library. This gentleman, an ecclesiastic and a member of the Senate, has so high a character for learning and honesty, that, though a partisan politician and a member of the opposition to the new government, he preserves (a rare thing in Peru) the respect and confidence of all. He placed the books of the library at my disposal and kindly selected for me those that would be of service.

The sources of information, however, were small and unsatisfactory. The military expeditions into the country to the eastward of the Andes left little or no reliable traces of their labors.

* A non-alcoholic beverage made by steeping the leaves of a native herb in boiling water. *H.B.*

The records of the explorations of the Jesuits were out of my reach, in the archives of Quito, and nearly all that I could get at were some meagre accounts of the operations of the Franciscans.

Though the information obtained in Lima was not great, I still think that a slight historical sketch of the attempts to explore the Montaña * of Peru, made since the conquest of that country by Pizarro, will not be uninteresting. According to one historian, Garcilasso de la Vega, himself a descendant of the Incas, the attention of the Peruvian government was directed to the country east of the Andes even before the time of the Spanish conquest. The sixth Inca, Rocca, sent his son Yahuar Huaccac at the head of 15,000 men, with three generals as companions and advisors, to the conquest of the country to the northward and eastward of Cuzco, called Antisuyo, inhabited by Indians called Antis. The young prince added a space of thirty leagues in that direction to the dominions of his father, but could reach no further on account of the roughness of the country and the difficulties of the march. The tenth and great Inca, Yupanqui, sent an expedition of 10,000 men to pursue the conquest of Yahuar Huaccac. These reached the Montaña, and, embarking on rafts upon the great river Amarumayo,† fought their way through tribes called Chunchos till they arrived, with only 1,000 men, into the territory of tribes called Musus. Finding their numbers now too small for conquest, they persuaded these Indians that they were friends, and by

* Montaña is the name given by the Peruvians to any wooded country, monte being the Spanish term for a thick and tangled forest. As there is no other wooded country in Peru except to the eastward of the Andes, the term applies only to the eastern slope, and the level country at the base of the mountains, stretching as far as the borders of Brazil.

† As I shall have occasion, in speaking of routes, to refer again to this river, I would like to draw particular attention to it, simply stating here, however, that all who have penetrated into the Montaña to the northward and eastward of Cuzco agree in reporting a large and navigable river arrived at soon after clearing the skirts of the mountains. Different tribes of Indians inhabit its banks, and I presume it is on this account that so many different names—such as Amarumayo, Mano, Tono, Inambiri, Guariguari, Chachiuara, and Madre-de-dios—have been given it. (It is now known as the Madre de Dios. *H.B.*)

3

their superior civilization obtained such an ascendency among them that the Musus agreed to send ambassadors to render homage and worship to the "Child of the Sun" and gave these men of the Inca race their daughters in marriage and a place in their tribe.

Years afterwards, during the reign of Huaynal Capac, the Incas and their descendants desired to return to Cuzco; but in the midst of their preparations they received intelligence of the downfall of their nation, and settled finally among the Musus, who adopted many of the laws, customs, usages, and worship of the Incas.

Love of dominion and power had induced the Indian princes of Peru to waste their treasures and the lives of their subjects in the subjugation of the Montaña. A stronger passion was now to urge a stronger people, the Spaniards, in the same direction. Stories of great empires, filled with large and populous cities whose streets were paved with gold; of a lake of golden sand; of a gilded king, who, when he rose in the morning, was smeared with oil and covered with gold dust blown upon him by his courtiers through long reeds, and of immense mineral and vegetable treasures had for some time filled the ears and occupied the minds of the avaricious conquerors.

Hernando Pizarro fitted out two expeditions, giving to Pedro de Candia the command of the first and to Pedro Anzulo that of the second. These men, led on by the report of the Indians, who constantly asserted that the rich countries they sought lay yet farther to the eastward, penetrated, it is supposed, as far as the Beni; * but, overcome by danger, privation, and suffering, they returned with no results, save marvellous stories of what they had seen and learned, which inflamed the curiosity and cupidity of others. These parties were generally accompanied by an ecclesiastic, who was the historian of the expedition. Some idea may be formed of the worthlessness of their records by examining a few of the stories related by them. Here is one:

"Juan Alvarez Maldonado made an expedition from Cuzco in

* A river in northern Bolivia. *H.B.*

4

the year 1561. He descended the eastern range of the Andes, and had scarcely cleared the rough and rocky ground of the slope when his party encountered two pigmies. They shot the female, and the male died of grief six days afterwards.

"Following the course of the great river Mano downwards, at the distance of two hundred leagues they landed upon a beach, and a band of soldiers penetrated into the woods. They found the trees so tall as to exceed an arrow-shot in height and so large that six men, with joined hands, could scarcely circle them. Here they found lying upon the ground a man, five yards in height, members in proportion, long snout, projecting teeth, vesture of beautiful leopard skin, short and shrivelled, and, for a walking-stick, a tree, which he played with as with a cane. On his attempting to rise, they shot him dead, and returned to the boat to give notice to their companions. These went to the spot, and found traces of his having been carried off. Following the track towards a neighboring hill, they heard thence such shouts and vociferations that they were astounded, and, horror-stricken, fled."

This is but one sample of the kind of stories which, inflaming the cupidity of the Spaniards, led them to brave the perils of the wilderness in search of El Dorado. I do not imagine, however, that they are broad lies. The soldiers of Maldonado evidently mistook monkeys for pigmies and some beast of the forest, probably the tapir, for a giant. Moreover, some of the Spaniards did find to the eastward of Cuzco a country answering, in some degree, to the description of the fabulous El Dorado. They penetrated into the valleys of Carabaya and found there washings of gold of great value. They subjugated the Indians; built the towns of San Juan del Oro, San Gaban, Sandia, etc.; and sent large quantities of gold to Spain. On one occasion they sent a mass of gold in the shape of an ox's head, and of the weight of two hundred pounds, as a present to Charles V. The Emperor, in acknowledgment, gave the title of "Royal City" to the town of San Juan del Oro, and ennobled its inhabitants. The Indians, however, in the course of time, revolted, murdered their oppres-

5

sors, and destroyed their towns. Up to the last three years this has been a sealed country to the white man. I shall have occasion to refer to it again.

While these efforts to penetrate the Montaña to the eastward of Cuzco were being made, Gonzalo Pizarro fitted out at Quito an expedition consisting of 350 Spaniards and 4,000 Indians, with large supplies of provisions and live stock. All who have read the brilliant pages of Prescott know the history of this expedition: the discovery of cinnamon; the treachery of Orellana; and the origin of the present name of the great river.

The failure of this expedition, and the almost incredible sufferings of the party who composed it, could not deter the Spaniards from their search for El Dorado. In 1560 the Marquis of Cañete, Viceroy of Peru, sent Pedro de Ursoa with a large company on this mission. This officer marched northward from Cuzco and embarked upon the Huallaga. At Lamas, a small town near that river, he was murdered by his lieutenant, Lope de Aguirre, who determined to prosecute the enterprise. Aguirre descended the Huallaga—and the Amazon to its mouth—coasted along the shores of Guiana and Venezuela, and took possession of the small island of Marguerita. There raising a party, he landed at Cumaná, with the purpose of conquering an empire on the mainland. He was, however, defeated by some Spanish troops who had already possession of the country, taken prisoner, carried to Trinidad, and hung.

Aguirre appears to have been a bold and violent man. His letter to Philip II, published in Humboldt's narrative, is indicative of his character. He says, "On going out of the river Amazon we landed at an island called La Margaretta. We there received news from Spain of the great faction of the Lutherans. This news frightened us exceedingly. We found among us one of that faction; his name was Monteverde. I had him cut in pieces, as was just; for, believe me, signor, wherever I am, people live according to the law."

6

The following story, from the *Viagero Universal* of Ulloa, shows his barbarity in yet more revolting colors. It appears that in all his marches he carried with him a favorite daughter. When defeated and surrounded, so that escape was impossible, he called this lady, and addressing her, said: "I had hoped to make thee a queen. This now is impossible. I cannot bear that you should live to be pointed at as the child of a traitor and a felon. Thou must prepare for death at my hands." She requested a few minutes for prayer, which was granted; but her father, thinking she was too long at her devotions, fired upon her whilst on her knees. The unfortunate lady staggered towards him; but taking her by the hand as she approached, the villain plunged his knife into her bosom, and she sank at his feet, murmuring, *Basta Padre Mio*— "It is enough, my father."

It is not to be expected that information of an exact and scientific character should be had from the voyages of adventurers like these. They were mere soldiers, and too much occupied in difficulties of travel, conflicts with Indians, ambitious designs, and internal dissentions, to make any notes of the topography or productions of the countries they passed through.

On the 4th of April, 1851, Lieutenant Lardner Gibbon of the navy arrived at Lima and delivered me my orders from the Navy Department, of which the following is a copy:

Navy Department, February 15, 1851
Sir: The department is about to confide to you a most important and delicate duty. The government desires to be put in possession of certain information relating to the valley of the river Amazon, in which term is included the entire basin, or watershed, drained by that river and its tributaries. This desire extends not only to the present condition of that valley, with regard to the navigability of its streams, but also to its capacities for cultivation and to the character and extent of its undeveloped commercial resources, whether of the field, the forest, the river, or the mine.

You will, for the purpose of obtaining such information, proceed across the Cordillera and explore the Amazon from its source to its mouth. Passed Midshipman Lardner Gibbon, a prudent and intelligent officer, has been selected to accompany you on this service, and is instructed to report accordingly. This, together with a few instruments necessary for such an expedition, will be delivered to you by him. Being joined by him, you will commence to make such arrangements as may be necessary for crossing the Andes and descending the Amazon; and having completed them, you will then proceed on your journey without further orders.

The route by which you may reach the Amazon river is left to your discretion. Whether you will descend the Ucayali, or the Huallaga, or any other of the Peruvian tributaries, or whether you will cross over into Bolivia and embark on the Mamoré or Ytenes, or whether you will try the Beni or any other route to the Madeira, and thence to the Amazon, the information which you collected under a former order will enable you to decide more judiciously than it is possible for the department, with the meagre state of its information upon the subject, to do. However, it is not desired that you should select any route by which you and your party would be exposed to savage hostility beyond your means of defence and protection.

Neither is it desirable that your party should be so large, on the one hand, as to excite the suspicion of the people, or give offence to the authorities, of the country through which you may pass, nor so small, on the other, as to endanger its success. You are, therefore, authorized to employ a cook, servant, guide and interpreter, and to provide them with such arms as it is customary only for travellers generally, in that part of the world, to carry for their own protection. And these arms you will have returned to you at Pará. The Navy Agent at Lima has been instructed to furnish, upon your requisition, the necessary articles for the outfit of yourself and party, and to honor your draft for a sum not exceeding five thousand dollars to cover your expenses by the way. As these expenses will be mostly for mules and arrieros, boats and boats' crews, it is supposed that the sum named will be much more than sufficient. You will use of it only for the necessary expenses of the party.

You will make such geographical and scientific observations by the way as may be consistent with the main object of the expedition, always bearing in mind that these are merely incidental, and that no part of the main objects of the expedition is to be interfered with by them. It is desirable that you should bring home with you specimens or samples of the various articles of produce from the Amazon river, together with such seeds or plants as might probably be introduced into this country with advantage. Arriving at Pará, you will embark by the first opportunity for the United States, and report in person to this department.

Wishing you a pleasant journey and a safe return to your country and friends,

I am, respectfully, your obedient servant,

WILL. A. GRAHAM

As the choice of route was thus left to my discretion, this, in connexion with the best and most efficient mode of carrying out my instructions, became an object of much consideration with me. As I had some time previously received intimation of the intention of the department to issue such orders, whilst in Valparaiso and Santiago I had sought what information was to be had there, and conversed with many persons regarding the routes through Bolivia and the navigability of the Bolivian tributaries of the Amazon. Two interesting routes presented themselves through this country : one by the river Mamoré and the other by the river Beni, a tributary of the Madeira, which is one of the main branches of the Amazon.

I was so much impressed with the importance of this latter route that I left Lima undecided whether I should take it or not; and at Tarma, after long and anxious deliberation (the measure being supported by Mr. Gibbon's advice and earnest personal solicitation), I determined to take the responsibility of dividing the party, and did so, furnishing Mr. Gibbon with a set of written instructions and verbally calling his attention to the river Beni.

Other reasons that induced me to take this step were that I might carry out the instructions of the department as fully as lay in my power; and while I gave my own personal attention to the countries drained by the upper Marañon and its tributaries, Mr. Gibbon might explore some, and gather all the information he could respecting others, of the Bolivian tributaries of the Amazon. I felt that, under my instructions requiring me to explore the Amazon from its source to its mouth, I could not neglect the route I finally determined to take. This route would enable me to form a judgment respecting the practicability of a transitable connexion between Lima and the navigable headwaters of the tributaries of the Amazon—would lead me through the richest and most productive mineral district of Peru—would put under my observation nearly all the course of the Amazon—and would enable me to gather information regarding the Pampa del Sacramento, or great plain, shut in between four great rivers, and concerning which it has been said, ''the two continents of America do not contain another country so favorably situated, or so fertile.''

That the rains might be entirely over and the roads on the mend, I fixed upon the 20th of May as the day of departure, and Mr. Gibbon and I set about making the necessary preparations. I engaged the services of Don Manuel Ijurra, a young Peruvian who had made the voyage down the Amazon a few years before, as interpreter. Capt. Gauntt, of the frigate *Raritan*, then lying in the harbor of Callao, was kind enough to permit a young master's mate from his ship, named Richards, to sign up with our party, besides supplying me with carbines, pistols, ammunition, and a tent. Capt. Magruder, of the *St. Mary*, another ship in the harbor, also offered me anything that his vessel could supply.

Our purchases were four saddle-mules, which we were fortunate enough to get young, sound, and well bitted, out of a drove just in from the mountains. We consulted the learned in such matters on the propriety of having them shod, and found the doctors disagreeing upon this subject very much. As they were from the mountains, and their hoofs were round, sound, and apparently as hard as iron, we decided not to shoe. We also purchased about a thousand yards of coarse cotton cloth, made in the mills at Lima and put up for mountain travel in bales of half a mule-load, hatchets, knives, tinder-boxes, fish-hooks, beads, looking-glasses, cotton handkerchiefs, ribbons, and cheap trinkets, which we thought might take the fancy of the Indians and purchase us services and food when money would not. These things were also put up in boxes of the same size and shape, and each equal to half a mule-load. Our trunks were arranged in the same way, so that they might be lashed one on each side of the mule's back, with an India-rubber bag (also obtained from the *Raritan*), which carried our bed-clothes, put on top in the space between them. Such small, incongruous articles as our pots and pans for cooking, our tent and particularly the tent-pole, which was carried fore and aft above a cargo and which, from its length, was poking into everything and constantly getting awry, gave us more trouble than anything else.

Our bedding consisted of the saddle-cloths, a stout blanket, and anything else that could be conveniently packed. An Englishman from New York, whom I met in Lima, gave me a soft coverlet made of the skins of a kind of racoon, which served me many a good turn ; and often, when in the cold of the Cordillera I wrapped myself in its warm folds, I felt a thrill of gratitude for the thoughtful kindness which had provided me with such a comfort. We purchased thick flannel shirts, *ponchos* of India-rubber, wool, and cotton, and had straw hats, covered with oil-cloth and fitted with green veils, to protect our eyes from the painful affections which often occur by the sudden bursting out of the sunlight upon the masses of snow that lie forever upon the mountain tops.

We carried two small kegs—one containing brandy, for drinking, and the other the common rum of the country, called *Ron de Quemar*, for burning—also, some coarse knives, forks, spoons, tin cups, and plates. I did not carry, as I should have done, a few cases of preserved meat, sardines, cheese, &c., which would have given us a much more agreeable meal than we often got on the road; but I did carry, in some India-rubber bags I also purchased, quite a large quantity of biscuit, which I had baked for me in Lima and which lasted us to Tarma.

We had the mules fitted with the heavy, deep-seated box saddles of Peru. I believe the English saddle would be much more comfortable, but it would be almost impossible with these to preserve the skin of the mule from chafe. The Peruvian saddles rest entirely upon the ribs of the animal, which are protected by at least six yards of a coarse woolen fabric manufactured in the country, called *jerga*, and touch the back-bone nowhere. These saddles are a wooden box frame, stuffed thickly on the inside, and covered outwardly with buckskin. They are fitted with heavy, square, wooden stirrups, which are intended to keep the legs from contact with projecting rocks and, being lined with fur, to keep the feet warm. There is also a heavy breast-strap and crupper for steep ascents and descents; and a thick *pillon*, or mat, made of thrums of cotton, silk, or hair, is thrown over the saddle to make the seat soft. Our guns, in leathern cases, were slung to the crupper, and the pistols carried in holsters, made with large pockets, to carry powder-flasks, percussion caps, and specimens that we might pick up on the road. A small box of instruments for skinning birds and dissecting animals; a medicine chest, containing among other things some arsenical soap for preserving skins; a few reams of coarse paper for drying leaves and plants; chart paper in a tin case; passports and other papers, also in a tin case; note-books, pencils, &c., completed our outfit. A chest was made, with compartments for the sextant, artificial horizon, boiling-point apparatus, camera lucida, and spy-glass. The chronometer was carried in the pocket, and the barometer, slung in a leathern case made for it, at the saddle-bow of Mr. Gibbon's mule.

On the 15th of May I engaged the services of an *arriero,* or muleteer. He engaged to furnish beasts to carry the party and its baggage from Lima to Tarma at ten dollars the head, stopping on the road wherever I pleased, and as long as I pleased, for that sum. An ordinary train of baggage mules may be had on the same route for about seven dollars the head. The arrieros of Peru, as a class, have a very indifferent reputation for faithfulness and honesty, and those on the route (that from Lima to Cerro Pasco) to which my friend particularly belonged are said to be the worst of their class. He was a thin, spare, dark Indian, of the *Sierra* or mountain land, about forty-five years of age, with keen, black eye, thin moustache, and deliberate in his speech and gesture. I thought I had seldom seen a worse face, and he managed to cheat me very soon after our acquaintance.

Arrieros, when they supply as many mules as I had engaged, always furnish a *peon,* or assistant, to help load and unload and take care of the mules. Mine, taking advantage of my ignorance in these matters, said to me that his peon was *desanimado* (disheartened), afraid of the *Piedra Parada,* or upright rock, where we were to cross the Cordillera, and had backed out; but that he himself could very well attend to the mules if I would be good enough to let him have the occasional assistance of my Indian servant. I unwarily promised, which was the cause of a good deal of difficulty; but when the old rascal complained of over-work and sickness on the road, I had an answer for him which always silenced him—which was that it was his own cupidity and dishonesty which caused it, and that if he did not work and behave himself, I would discharge him without pay and send back to Lima for another.

I directed him to bring the mules to the hotel door on the 20th. Upon his finding that this was a Tuesday, he demurred, saying that it was an unlucky day and that no arriero was willing to start on that day, but that Monday was lucky, and begged that I would be ready by then. This I could not do. On Wednesday, the 21st of May, we loaded up, though I had to cajole and finally

13

to bribe the old fellow to take on all the baggage, which he represented to be too much for his beasts.

I did wrong to start, for the party was short of a servant. (I had not been able to get one in Lima, except at an unreasonable price, and depended upon getting one in some of the towns of the Sierra.) The arriero needed a peon, and the mules were overloaded. I would strongly advise all travellers in these parts to imitate the conduct of the Jesuits, whose first day's journey is to load their burden mules; saddle and mount their riding-mules; go twice round the patio, or square, on the inside of their dwelling to see that everything is prepared and fits properly; and then unload and wait for the morning. However, I foresaw a longer delay by unloading again than I was willing to make. After a hard morning's work in drumming up the Peruvian part of the expedition (these people have not the slightest idea that a man will start on a journey on the day he proposes), the party, consisting of myself, Mr. Gibbon, Mr. Richards, Mr. Ijurra, Mauricio, an Indian, and the arriero, Pablo Luis Arrendondo, with seven burden-mules, defiled out by the Gate of Marvels (*Puerta de Maravillas*) and took the broad and beaten road that ascends the left bank of the Rimac.

Our course lay over an apparently level and very stony road. To the right were green cane and alfalfa fields and on the left and behind, the vegetation afforded by the valley of the Rimac; but ahead all was barren, grim, and forbidding.

Shortly before sunset we stopped at the hacienda (estate, farm, or settlement) of Santa Clara and applied for pasturage. We were told by an old Negro woman sitting on the ground at the door of the house that there was none, which was confirmed by two men who just then rode up and who expressed their regret at not being able to accommodate us. It was remarkable to see such poverty and squalid wretchedness nine miles from the great city of Lima; it was like passing in a moment from the most luxurious civilization into savage barbarity—from the garden to

14

the desert. We rode on, about three miles further, to another hacienda, where we arrived at half-past six o'clock P.M.

Before the mules could be unloaded, it became very dark, so that the arriero and Mauricio had considerable trouble in driving them to the pasturage. Indeed some of them got away. I could hear them galloping furiously up and down the road, and I went to bed (on a table in the only room in the house) with the comfortable reflection that I had balked at starting and should have to return or send back to Lima to buy more mules. Tormented with these reflections and oppressed with the excitement and fatigue of the day, I could not sleep. I tossed about until just before daylight, when, as I was finally dropping off to sleep, a couple of game cocks, tied by the leg in the room, commenced their salutation to the morn and screamed out their clarion notes within a yard of my ear. This was too much for me. I rushed out to meet a heavenly morning, and old Luis, with the intelligence that the mules were "all right." I took off my upper clothes and plunged head, neck, and shoulders into the water of a little mountain stream that rushed clear and cold as ice by the roadside in front of the house. Thus refreshed and invigorated, the appearance of affairs took a new aspect, and light-heartedness and hope came back as strong and fresh as in the days of boyhood.

The mayordomo, or steward of the estate, was a Chino (descendant of Indian and Negro) and seemed an amiable and intelligent fellow. He gave us a supper of *chupe*; * and whilst we were eating it, he engaged himself in teaching the children of a neighbor the multiplication table and the catechism.

The house was built of adobe, or sun-dried bricks, and roofed with tiles. It had but one room, which was the general receptacle for all comers. A mud projection, of two feet high and three wide, stood out from the walls of the room all round and served as a

* Chupe, during the time of Herndon's visit, was a universal article of diet in the Peruvian Sierra. It was a broth, or soup, made generally of potatoes, cheese, and lard. Sometimes meat was boiled in it. *H.B.*

15

standing bed-place for numbers. Others laid their blankets and ponchos and stretched themselves upon the floor, so that, with whites, Indians, Negroes, trunks, packages, horse furniture, game cocks, and guinea pigs, we had quite a caravanserai appearance.

The supper and bed that the steward had given us were gratuitous; he would accept no remuneration. We got our breakfast of chupe and eggs at a *tambo* or roadside inn nearly opposite. Though we commenced loading up soon after daylight, we did not get off until half-past nine. Such delays were invariable; this was owing to the want of a peon and another servant.

CHAPTER II

*   *   *

May 22. Roads still good; valley gradually narrowing, and hills becoming higher and more barren and rocky. We passed several squads of asses and llamas carrying potatoes and eggs to Lima. Six miles from Pacayar is the village, or *pueblo,* of Chaclacayo, consisting of four or five houses constructed of cane and mud. Soon after leaving this, the stream approached the hills so close that there was no longer room between them for the road, which had to be cut out of the side of the hill. It was very narrow and seemed in some places to overhang the stream fifty feet below it. Just as we were turning an angle of the road, we met a man driving two horses before him, which immediately mingled in with our burden mules and endangered their going over the precipice.

Our arriero shouted to the man, and spurring his horse through the mules, commenced driving back the horses of the other, who flourished his whip and insisted upon passing. I expected to see a fight and mischief happen, which would probably have fallen upon us, as the other had nothing to lose, when Ijurra called out to him and represented that our cargoes were very valuable and that if one were lost he should be held responsible; whereupon he desisted, drove his horses back, and suffered us to pass. This caused us to be more careful in our march. I sent Gibbon, with Richards, ahead to warn persons, or give us warning, in time to prevent a collision.

17

At 2 P.M. we stopped at the tambo of Yanacoto. I determined to stay here a day or two to get things shaken into their places. We pitched the tent in the valley before the road and proceeded to make ourselves as comfortable as possible. There seemed to be no cultivation in this valley, which here is about half a mile wide. It is covered with bushes, except close to the water's edge, where grow reeds and flags. The bushes are dwarf willow and a kind of locust called *Sangre de Cristo,* which bears a broad bean containing four or five seeds and a pretty red flower, something like our crêpe myrtle. There is also a bush, of some ten or twelve feet in height, called *Molle.* This is the most common shrub of the country and has a wider climatic range than any other of this slope of the Andes. It has long, delicate leaves, like the acacia, and produces an immense quantity of small red berries in large bunches.

May 24. About four and a half miles above Yanacoto, which we left this morning, we passed the little village of San Pedro Mama, where the first bridge is thrown over the Rimac. Heavy, rough stonework is built on each side of the river, into which are inserted massive pieces of timber, standing out a few feet from the face of the masonry and hewn flat on top. On their ends are laid trunks of trees, crossing the river, and securely lashed. Athwart these are laid sticks of wood, of some two or three inches diameter, lashed down and covered over with bundles of reeds, mud, and stones.

Near Cocachacra, where we arrived in the late afternoon, we saw well-tilled fields, green with alfalfa and corn. We pitched the tent in a meadow near the river and outside the town for the purpose of avoiding company and disagreeable curiosity. Although we had seen fields of corn before entering the village, we could get none for our mules after we got there. To every inquiry for hay, fodder, or grain, the constant reply was *"No hay"* (there is none). Gibbon, however, persevered until some one told him in an undertone, as if imparting a great secret, where a little corn was to be purchased, and he got a peck or two.

18

Cocachacra is a village of about one hundred inhabitants and at present the residence of the sub-prefect or governor of the province, which is that of Huarochiri. This province, according to the *Guia de Forasteros* (a sort of official almanac published yearly at Lima), is conterminous with that of Lima and commences at eighteen miles from the city.

We called on the sub-prefect and exhibited our Peruvian passports, asking, at the same time, that he give us some assistance in obtaining food for our beasts. This he seemed lukewarm about and I did not press him, for I had made up my mind that as far as it was possible I would avoid appealing to authority for the purpose of obtaining supplies, and go without what I could not buy or beg. We slept comfortably in the tent. Nights getting cool.

May 25. Started at 10 A.M. Valley getting so narrow as not to allow room for the road, which is in many places cut from the rock on the side of the hill, very narrow, rough, and precipitous, rising and falling as it crosses the spurs of the hills. We passed on the road the ruins of an ancient Indian town; the houses had been small, built of stone on terraces cut from the mountain-side. At 5 P.M., we arrived at the chacra of Moyoc, belonging to Señor Ximines, an old gentleman of Lima who had made a large fortune by mining. Here we pitched for the night, having travelled about fifteen miles, which is our usual day's journey. This is a most beautiful little dell, entirely and closely surrounded by mountains.

The steward of Ximenes, a nice old fellow with a young, pretty wife, gave us, at a reasonable price, pasturage for the beasts and a capital chupe. We saw here, for the first time, a vegetable of the potato kind called *Oca*. It resembles in appearance the Jerusalem artichoke, though longer and slimmer; boiled or roasted it is very agreeable to the taste. Richards compared its flavor to that of green corn; I suggested pumpkin, and he allowed that it was between the two. Gibbon shot a pair of beautiful small wild ducks that were gambolling in the Rimac and shooting the rapids with the speed of an arrow.

19

May 26. The river is now reduced to a mountain torrent, raging in foam over the debris of the porphyritic cliffs, which overhang its bed for hundreds of feet in height. The valley still occasionally widens out and gives room for a little cultivation. Where this is the case, it is generally bounded on one side or the other by cliffs of sandstone, in which innumerable parrots have perforated holes for nests, and the road at these places lies broad and level at their base. We crossed the river frequently on such bridges as I have already described and arrived at San Mateo at half-past 5 P.M., having travelled only twelve miles. We pitched in an old and abandoned alfalfa field above the town and got supper from the postmaster.

May 27. The town of San Mateo is situated on both sides of the Rimac at an elevation of ten thousand two hundred feet. The men work the fields of maize, potatoes, and beans; the women do all the household work, besides carrying their meals to the workmen on the farms, over hills that would make a lazy man shudder even to look at.

The costume of the Serrana women is different from that of the women of the coast. It consists of a very narrow skirt and a body of coarse woolen cloth, generally blue, which comes from Lima and is belted around the waist with a broad-figured woolen belt, woven by themselves. A woolen apron with a figured border is worn on the left side, hanging from the right shoulder by a strap, and in the cold of the morning and evening the shoulders are covered with a thick, colored blanket, reaching to the hips. A high, broad-brimmed straw-hat, with shoes of raw-hide, drawn with a string around the ankle, and no stockings complete the costume. These people seem contented with what they have and don't want money. It was with great difficulty we could persuade them to sell us anything, always denying that they had it. Mr. Gibbon, being suddenly sick with chills and fever, could not eat the chupe, which had, at first, been made with *charqui,* or jerked beef, but which has now dwindled down to cheese and potatoes. I made a speech to some curious loafers about the tent, in which

20

HACIENDA DE MAYOC

Wagner & Mc Guigans Lith.Phila.

I appealed to their pride and patriotism, telling them that I thought it strange that so large a town as San Mateo, belonging to so famous a country as Peru, could not furnish a sick stranger, who could eat nothing else, with a few eggs. Whereupon, a fellow went off and brought us a dozen, though he had just sworn by the Pope that there were no such things in the village.

May 28. Mr. Gibbon and I, guided by a boy, rode over to the hacienda of San José de Párac, leaving Richards and Ijurra in charge of the camp. The ride occupied about three hours, over the worst roads, bordered by the highest cliffs and deepest ravines, we had yet seen. The earth here shows her giant skeleton bare: mountains of granite, rather than rocks, rear their gray heads to the skies. I brought letters to Don Torribio Malarin, the superintendent of the mines, who received us kindly and entertained us with much hospitality. His house was comfortably heated with a stove, and the chamber furnished with a large four-post bedstead and the biggest and heaviest bureau I had ever seen. I was somewhat surprised at the sight of these—they must have come up in pieces, for nothing so large could have been fastened on a mule's back or passed entire in the narrow parts of the road.

May 29. Accompanied by Don Torribio, we visited the mines. They are much nearer San Mateo then is the hacienda, but there is no road to them from that village. The road, or rather path, lay along the side of the mountain and zigzagged up and down to turn precipices, now running near the banks of the little stream and now many hundreds of feet above it. The ride was bad enough at this time—it must be frightful in the rainy season. The mine called Santa Rosa, which we went into, has a perpendicular depth of five hundred and twenty feet, that is, the bottom of the shaft, which penetrates the mountain at an angle of about twenty-five degrees, is five hundred and twenty feet below the mouth of it. The superincumbent earth frequently requires to be supported by beams of wood laid against each other in the form of a Gothic arch. Don Torribio told us that he had instructed the workmen not to blast while we were in the mine, because the dreadful

23

reverberation of sound often had an unhappy effect upon people not accustomed to it—which, as we were men who sometimes dealt in heavy artillery, we did not thank him for.

Returning from the mine, we met a drove of llamas on their way from the hacienda. This is quite an imposing sight, especially when the drove is encountered suddenly at a turn of the road. The leader, which is always elected on account of his superior height, has his head decorated with tufts of colored woolen fringe, hung with little bells; and his extreme height (often six feet), gallant and graceful carriage, pointed ear, restless eye, and quivering lip, as he faces you for a moment, make him as striking an object as one can conceive. Upon pressing on him, he bounds aside, either up or down the cliff, and is followed by the herd, scrambling over places that would be impassable for the mule or the donkey.

They travel immense distances, but by short stages—not more than nine or ten miles per day. It is necessary, in long journeys, to have double the number required to carry the cargo, so as to give them relays. The burden of the llama is about one hundred and thirty pounds. He will not carry more and will be beat to death rather than move when he is overloaded or tired. The males only are worked; the females are kept for the breed. They appear gentle and docile, but when irritated they have a very savage look and spit at the object of their anger with great venom. The spittle is said to be very acrid and will raise blisters where it touches the skin. We saw none of these animals in the wild state. They are bred on the haciendas in great numbers. We had no opportunity of seeing the *guanaco* or *alpaca* (other varieties of the Peruvian sheep), though now and then, in crossing the mountains, we caught a glimpse of the wild and shy *vicuña*. These go in herds of ten or fifteen females accompanied by one male, who is ever on the alert. On the approach of danger he gives warning by a shrill whistle and his charge makes off with the speed of the wind.

June 1. Beautiful day. I returned with Gibbon to San Mateo, where I found Richards sick and the muleteer growling at the delay. We loaded up and got off at eleven. At twelve the valley narrowed to a dell of about fifty feet in width. The stream occupied its whole breadth, with the exception of a narrow, but smooth and level, mule-path on its right bank. This is a very remarkable place. On each side, the red porphyry rock rises perpendicularly for full five hundred feet. In places it overhangs the stream and road. The traveller feels as if he were passing through some tunnel of the Titans. The upper exit from the dell is so steep that steps have been cut in the rock for the mule's feet, and the stream rushes down the rock-obstructed declivity in foaming fury, flinging clouds of white spray over the traveller and rendering the path slippery and dangerous.

We stopped at four at the public inn of Acchahuarcu where we pitched and bought barley straw at the rate of twelve and a half cents the armful, called *tercio,* which is just enough for one mule. The mercury in the barometer being below the scale, we had to cut away the brass casing in front and mark the height of the column on the inside of the case with a pen-knife.

June 2. Got off at half-past ten. Road tolerably good and not very precipitous. At twelve we arrived on a level with the lowest line of snow. We were marking the barometer when a traveller rode up, who proved to be an old schoolmate of mine. I had not seen or even heard of him since we were boys. The meeting at this place was an extraordinary and very agreeable occurrence. It was also fortunate for me, for my friend was head machinist at the mines of Morococha and gave us a note to the administrator, which secured us a hospitable reception and an interesting day or two. Without this we should have been compelled to pass on, for pasturage here is very scant. The people of the mines have to pay a high price for their barley straw and are not willing to give it to every stray traveller. At 2 P.M. we arrived at the highest point of the road, called the pass of Antarangra, or copper rock.

Gibbon and I spurred our panting and trembling mules to the summit of the hill, and had nothing around us but snow, granite, and dark gray porphyry.

I was disappointed in the view from this place. The peaks of the Cordillera that were above us looked low and presented the appearance of a hilly country, at home, on a winter-day; while the contrast between the snowy hills and the bright green of lower ranges, together with the view of the placid little lakes which lie so snug and still in their midst, gave an air of quiet beauty to the scene very distinct from the savage and desolate grandeur I had expected. Gibbon sketched the Cordillera, while Richards lay shivering on the ground, enveloped in our blankets, a martyr to the *veta*.

Veta is the sickness caused by the rarity of the atmosphere at these great elevations. The Indians call it veta, or vein, because they believe it is caused by veins of metal diffusing a deadly poisonous infection. The affection displays itself in a violent headache, with the veins of the head swollen and turgid, a difficulty of respiration, and cold extremities. The smell of garlic is said to alleviate the symptoms, and the arrieros generally anoint their cattle over the eyes and on the forehead with an unguent made of tallow, garlic, and wild marjoram, as a preventive, before attempting the ascent. I did not observe that our animals were affected, though they trembled and breathed hard, which, I think, was attributable to the steepness of the hill up which we rode. The elevation was sixteen thousand and forty-four feet.

The road hence is cut along the flank of the mountain, at whose base lies a pretty little lake. Though not yet sixty miles from the sea, we had crossed the great "divide" which separates the waters of the Atlantic from those of the Pacific. The last steps of our mules had made a striking change in our geographical relations. I musingly dropped a bit of green moss plucked from the hill-side upon the placid waters of the little lake, and as it floated along I followed it, in imagination, down through the luxurious climes, the beautiful skies, and enchanting scenery of the tropics to the mouth of the great river; thence across the Caribbean sea, through the Yucatán pass, into the Gulf of Mexico; thence along the Gulf Stream; and so out upon the ocean, off the shores of Florida.

I was now, for the first time, fairly in the field of my operations. I had been sent to explore the Valley of the Amazon, to sound its streams, and to report as to their navigability. I was commanded to examine its fields, its forests, and its rivers that I might gauge their capabilities, active and dormant, for trade and commerce and make known the resources which lie in concealment there. Before us lay this immense field, dressed in the robes of everlasting summer and embracing an area of thousands upon thousands of square miles on which the footfall of civilized man had never been heard. Behind us towered, in forbidding grandeur, the crests and peaked summits of the Andes, clad in the garb of eternal winter. The contrast was striking, and the field inviting. But who were the laborers? Gibbon and I. We were all. Questions which I could not answer, and reflections which I could not keep back, crowded upon me. Oppressed with their weight and the magnitude of the task before me, I turned away lamenting my want of ability and sincerely regretting that the duty before me had not been assigned to abler hands.

CHAPTER III

* * *

We arrived at Morococha at 5 P.M. This is a copper mining hacienda, belonging to some German brothers named Pflücker, of Lima, who own, also, several silver mines in the neighborhood. The copper and silver of these mountains are intimately mixed. The mining business of the hacienda is conducted by a director, an intelligent and gentlemanly young German named Richard von Durfeldt, and its fiscal affairs and general business by an administrator, a fine-looking young Spaniard, Don José Fco. de Lizarralde, whose kindly courtesy we shall long remember.

The engineer, or machinist, is my old friend and schoolmate Shepherd, who seemed to be a "Jack of all trades"—blacksmith, carpenter, watch-maker, and doctor. His room was quite a curiosity. I never saw so many different things gathered together in so small a place: shelves of fine standard books; a dispensary for physic; all manner of tools, from the sledge-hammer and the whip-saw to the delicate instruments of the watch-maker; parts of watches lying under bell-glasses; engravings hanging around the walls, with a great chart, setting forth directions for the treatment of all manner of diseases and accidents; horse gear and saddle-bags; boots, shoes, and every variety of garment, from the heavy woolen poncho of the man to the more delicate cotton petticoat of the woman, for my friend has a pretty young Sierra wife, who took great pleasure in talking to me about the home and relations of my *paisano*. Shepherd's warm room and bed, with plenty of covering, was a princely luxury in that cold climate. These things are comparative, and I had not slept under a roof but twice since I left Lima. An old Englishman from the Isle of Guernsey, named Grant, who seemed to be a sort of factotum, who knew and did everything, and who was unwearied in his kindness and attention to us, made up the sum of our pleasant acquaintances at Morococha. We had beef and mutton for dinner, with good butter and cheese. Gibbon not well. Richards very sick and under treatment from Shepherd.

June 3. We went to see the Mountain of Puy-puy, said to be higher than Chimborazo. The place of view is about three miles from Morococha. We passed the openings of a copper and silver mine, and rode along a boggy country where turf is cut for fuel. We saw many snipes, ducks, and other aquatic birds. This upset all my preconceived notions. I had no idea that I should see, at fifteen thousand feet above the level of the sea, anything that would remind me of duck-shooting in the marshes of the Rappahannock. To see the mountain, it was necessary to cross a range of hills about seven or eight hundred feet in height. The road went up diagonally, and the ascent was the most toilsome operation I had ever undertaken. We were obliged to dismount, when about three-fourths of the way up, and lead the mules; the path was muddy and slippery, and we had to stop to blow at every half-dozen steps. Gibbon, who has now recovered, declared that this was the only occasion in which he had ever found the big spurs of the country of any service; for when he slipped and fell, as we all frequently did, he said that he should inevitably have gone to the bottom had he not dug his spurs into the soil and so held on. I think that I suffered more than any of the party. On arriving at the top, I was fairly exhausted; I thought my heart

29

would break from my breast with its violent agitation. I soon recovered, however, and was amply repaid by the splendor of the view. The lofty cone-shaped mountain, clad in its brilliant mantle from the top even to the cylindrical base upon which it rested, rose in solitary majesty from the plain beneath us; and when the sunlight, bursting from the clouds, rested upon its summit, it was beautiful, indeed. Gibbon almost froze making a sketch of it, and the rest of us tired ourselves nearly to death endeavoring to get a shot at a herd of shy vicuñas that were seen feeding among the distant rocks. We had a fatiguing ride back home, and enjoyed a late dinner and a good night's rest.

June 4. We took leave of our hospitable friends (whom I could no longer intrude our large party upon), and started at meridian, leaving Richards too sick to travel. We travelled over a heavy rolling country; the southern sides of the hills clothed with verdure and affording tolerable pasture; the northern sides bare and rocky—no trees or bushes. About nine miles from Morococha, we crossed a range of hills to the right, and entered the village of Pachachaca, a small place of two hundred inhabitants. The people seem more industrious than those of the villages on the other side. There are fine crops of barley here, and we saw cabbages, onions, peaches, and eggs in the shops. We were greater objects of curiosity in this place than we had been before. The people, I believe, took us for peddlers, and the woman from whom we got our supper and breakfast seemed offended because we would not sell her some candles, and importuned Gibbon for the sale of his straw hat. The men wore short woolen trousers, buttoned at the knee, together with, generally, two pairs of long woolen stockings. The trousers and stockings are woven in this neighborhood. Fuel is the *taquia,* or dried cattle manure. Gibbon and I had occasion afterwards to laugh at our fastidiousness in objecting to a mutton-chop broiled upon a coal of cow-dung.

June 5. We travelled down the valley about east. At about one and a half miles we passed a very curious-looking place, where a small stream came out of a valley to the northward and westward and spread itself over a flat table-rock, soft and calcareous. It poured over this rock in a sort of horse-shoe cataract and then spread over an apparently convex surface of this same soft rock, about two hundred and fifty yards wide, crossing the valley down which we were travelling. This rock sounded hollow under the feet of the mules, and I feared we should break through at every instant.

The valley about two miles from Pachachaca is cut across by rocky hills. Here we turned to the northward and eastward. The country at first offered some pasturage, but became more barren as we advanced, only showing, now and then, some patches of barley. At half-past two, after a ride over a stony and dusty plain, bordered on each side by rocky mountains, we arrived at the bridge of Oroya. The bridge consisted of four chains, of about a quarter of an inch diameter, stretched horizontally across the river from strong stone-work on each side. These are interlaced with thongs of hide; sticks of about one and a half inches in diameter are laid across them and lashed down, forming a floor. Two other chains are stretched across about four feet above these and connected with them by thongs of hide; these serve for balustrades and would prevent a mule from jumping off. The bridge was about fifty feet above the water when we passed. It seemed very light and rocked and swayed under the motion of the mules in crossing it. The heavy cargoes are taken off and carried over on the shoulders of the bridge-keeper and his assistants. The toll is twelve and a half cents the mule; and the same, the cargo. The bridge-keeper seemed astonished and somewhat annoyed when I told him that one of the cargoes, which he left on the mule, was the heaviest I had, being a box filled with bags of shot, balls, and powder, together with the specimens of ore and rocks we had collected.

The river at this place turns from its southern course and runs to the eastward, by the village of Oroya, where we camped. This village contains about one hundred inhabitants, though we saw only five or six men, most of the male inhabitants being away to the harvest on the plains above. The women seemed nearly all to be employed in spinning wool, holding the bundle of wool in the left hand and spinning it out by a hanging broach. Very few of them spoke Spanish, but a corrupt *Quichua,* or language of the Incas. We bought barley straw for the mules and got a beef chupe, with eggs and roasted potatoes, for ourselves. We saw some small trees within the deserted enclosures where houses had been, bearing a very fragrant flower, something resembling the heliotrope, but much larger and tinged with a reddish color. We also saw flocks of sheep, but got no mutton for dinner.

June 6. Got under way at 9 A.M. and made a considerable ascent for about two miles. We then rode over a plain, with rolling hills on each side, covered with a short grass giving pasturage to large flocks of sheep and some cows. The road then rose again, until, at half-past eleven, we stood at the head of a ravine leading down to the valley of Tarma. The height of this spot above the level of the sea was eleven thousand two hundred and seventy feet. We rode down this ravine for three-quarters of an hour, over a road filled with fragments of white calcareous rock. When nearly at the foot, the plants and flowers familiar to us on the other side began to make their appearance, and in such quick succession that it seemed that an hour's ride carried us over many a mile of the tedious ascent to the westward of the mountains. First appeared the hardy little flowers of the heights above San Mateo; then the barley; the alfalfa; the Indian corn; beans, turnips; shrubs, becoming bushes; bushes, trees; flowers growing larger and gayer in their colors (yellow predominating), till the pretty little city of Tarma, embosomed among the hills and enveloped in its covering of willows and fruit trees, with its long lawns of alfalfa (the greenest of grasses) stretching out in front, broke upon our view. The ride of today was a long and tiresome one, being mostly a bone-shaking descent. We hailed with pleasure the sight of the little town as a resting place, after the tedious passage of the Cordillera, and felt that one of the inconveniences and perils of the expedition was safely and happily passed.

We arrived at 4 P.M., and rode straight to the house of a gentleman, Don Lorenzo Burgos, to whom I brought a letter of introduction from friend Shepherd of Morococha; which letter contained the modest request that Don Lorenzo should place his house at my disposal. This he acceded to without hesitation, removing his sick wife, in spite of remonstrance, into another room, and giving us his hall for our baggage, and his chamber for our sleeping room. This I would not have acceded to, except that this is not Don Lorenzo's place of residence, but a new house which he is constructing here, and which he is only staying at for a few days till his wife is able to travel to their regular place of residence. There is no public house in the town and it is customary to take travellers in. When I (next morning) presented a letter of introduction from the Bishop of Eretria to the Cura of Tarma, his first question was, "Where are you lodged?" And when I told him, he seemed annoyed, and said that I had not treated him properly in not coming to his house. Don Lorenzo gave us some dinner, and we slept well after the fatigues of the day.

Tarma, a town of some seven thousand inhabitants, belonging to the province of Pasco and department of Junin, is beautifully situated in an amphitheatre of mountains which are clothed nearly to the top with waving fields of barley. The valley in front, about half a mile wide and two miles long, appears level, and is covered with the greenest and richest pasturage. Its borders are fringed with fruit trees, and the stream which waters it plunges, in a beautiful little cataract of some thirty feet in height, over a ledge of rocks at the farther end. Its climate is delicious; it is the resort of sickly people from Lima and the cold and inclement mining districts, who find comfort and restoration in its pure atmosphere and mild and equable temperature.

The houses of Tarma are built of adobe and the better sort are whitewashed within and without, floored with gypsum and tiled. The wood and iron work is of the rudest possible description. The doors of the house we are living in very much resemble "bird's-eye maple.'' Some of the houses are partially papered, and carpeted with common Scotch carpeting. Most of them have *patios,* or enclosed squares within, and some of them flat roofs, with a parapet around them, where maize, peas, beans, and such things are placed in the sun to dry.

Sunday is the great market-day. The market-place is filled with country people, who come in to sell their manufactures of ponchos, blankets, shoes, and hats (made of vicuña wool), and to buy coca,* cotton goods, and *aguadiente,* as well as to attend mass and get drunk. It is quite a busy and animated scene. The men are generally dressed in tall straw hats, ponchos, breeches buttoned at the knee, and long woolen stockings; the women, in a blue woolen skirt tied around the waist and open in front to show a white cotton petticoat, the shoulders covered with a mantle consisting of two or three yards of gay-colored plush, called *Bayeta de Castilla,* or Spanish baize. Everything foreign in this country is called *de Castilla* (of Castile), as in Brazil, it is called *da Rainha* (of the Queen). The skirt of a lady of higher quality consists of a colored print or mousseline. She rarely, unless dressed for company, takes the trouble to put on the bodice of her dress, which hangs down behind, and is covered with a gay shawl, passed around the bust, with the end thrown gracefully over the left shoulder. The hair, particularly on Sundays, is in perfect order; parted in the middle and hanging down in two plaits behind. It is surmounted by a very neat, low-crowned straw-hat, the crown

* The dried leaves of the coca-plant, from which cocaine is derived, has been used by the Peruvian Indians since most ancient times. Employed as an offering to the sun, it was used to produce smoke at the great sacrifices; the priests, it was believed, must chew it during the ceremonies; otherwise the gods would not be propitiated. Herndon gives this description of it: "*Coca* is a bush of about four feet high, producing a small light-green leaf, which is the part used. The blossom is white, and the fruit a small red berry. The leaf of this plant is to the Indian of Peru what tobacco is to our laboring classes in the South—a luxury which has become a necessity. Supplied with an abundance of it, he sometimes performs prodigies of labor, and can go without food for several days. Without it, he is miserable and will not work." *H.B.*

34

being nearly covered with a broad ribbon. The women are generally large and well developed; not very pretty, but with amiable, frank, and agreeable manners; they have, almost invariably, a pleasant smile, with an open and engaging expression of countenance.

Religion flourishes in Tarma and the Cura seems to have a busy time of it. I think that no day passed while we were here that there was not a *fiesta*. These, in Tarma, are generally celebrated with music, ringing of bells, firing of rockets, and dances of Indians. A dozen vagabonds are dressed in what is supposed to be the costume of the ancient Indians. This consists of a red blanket hanging from one shoulder and a white one from the other, reaching nearly to the knee and girded around the waist; the usual short blue breeches, with a white fringe at the knee; stockings of an indifferent color, and shoes or sandals of rawhide, gathered over the toes with a draw-string and tied around the ankles. The head-dress is a low-crowned, broad-brimmed round hat made of wool and surrounded with a circlet of dyed feathers of the ostrich. Thus costumed, the party march through the streets, stopping every now and then to execute a sort of dance to the melancholy and monotonous music of a reed pipe, accompanied by a rude flat drum—both in the hands of the same performer. Each man has a stick or club of hard wood and a very small wooden or hide shield, which he strikes with the club at certain periods of the dance, making a low clattering in time with the music. They have also small bells, called *cascabeles*, attached to the knees and feet, which jingle in the dance. They and their company of Indians and Mestizos smell very badly on a near approach.

June 7. I suffered all day with violent pain in the head and limbs, caused by the ride of yesterday. These Peruvian saddles, though good for the beasts, and for riding up and down hill, stretch the legs so far apart as to give the unaccustomed rider severe pains in the muscles of the thighs. I had to ride a large portion of the distance with my leg over the pommel, like a lady.

35

We paid off and parted with the arriero, Pablo Luis Arredondo. I did not find him so great a rascal as I anticipated. Except for the disposition to get all out of me he could (which was very natural) and an occasional growl (which was also to be expected), I had no reason to be dissatisfied with Luis. Ijurra was always quarrelling with him, but I think Ijurra has the fault of his countrymen generally, and wants the temper and patience necessary to manage ignorant people. By soft words and some bribery, I got along well enough with the old fellow; and he loaded his mules beyond their usual cargoes and drove them along very well. I was frequently astonished at the difficulties they surmounted, loaded as they were. Our riding mules were perfect treasures. Sure-footed, steady, strong, and patient, they bore us along easily and with comfort; Gibbon says that he will part with his with tears when we are compelled to give them up and take to the boats.

We had a visit from the Cura, and went to see the sub-prefect of the province, a gentleman named Mier, who promised me such assistance as I needed in my visit to Chanchamayo. Both of these gentlemen earnestly deprecated the idea of trusting myself and party among the *Chunchos* Indians on the other side of the river Chanchamayo, saying that they were very hostile to the whites and dangerous.

June 11. We rode about a league down the valley which leads to Chanchamayo, to the farm of General Otero, to whom we brought letters of introduction. We found this farm a different sort of affair from anything we had hitherto seen in this way in our travels. This is in a high state of cultivation, well enclosed with mud walls, and in beautiful order. The general—a good-looking, farmer-like old gentleman—met us with great cordiality and showed us over the premises. He has a very large house with all the necessary offices attached, which he built himself. Indeed, he said he had made the farm; for when he purchased it, it was a stony and desolate place, and he had expended much time, labor, and money on it. There were two gardens: one for vegetables and fruit and one for flowers. They were both in fine order. The fruits were peaches of various kinds, apples, strawberries, almonds, and some few grapes. The flowers were principally roses, pinks, pansies, jessamines, and geraniums. Both fruit and flowers were of rather indifferent quality, but much better than one would expect to see in so elevated and cold a situation.

This being the harvest season, the general was gathering his crop of maize. About twenty peons or laborers were bringing it in from the fields and throwing it down in piles in a large court-yard, while boys and women were engaged in shucking it. In one corner of the square, under a snug little shed attached to one of the barns, with stone seats around it, sat the general's three daughters, sewing, and probably superintending the shucking. They were fair, sweet-looking girls. The general had a tray of glasses, with some cigars and also some *Italia* (a cordial made of a Muscatel grape that grows in the province of Ica, and also called Ica brandy) brought out for us. The whole place had a home look that was quite pleasing.

June 12. Dined with a countryman of ours who is living here, Dr. Buckingham, and a couple of young ladies, one of whom seemed to be his housekeeper. The dinner was after the Peruvian fashion: first, a sort of thick soup; then, roasted ribs of mutton, served with salad; this succeeded by a dish of stewed guinea pigs mixed with a variety of vegetables, and which would have been very good but for the addition of a quantity of *aji*, or red pepper, which made it unendurable to the unaccustomed palate, winding up with the invariable dessert of *dulces*, or sweetmeats. A Peruvian never thinks of taking water during dinner and always eats sweetmeats after dinner, that he may then safely take water; so that *Tomar dulces, para beber agua* is a sort of dietetic proverb with them.

June 16. We left Tarma for the Chanchamayo. This is the first time I have applied to authority for the means of locomotion. I did it inadvertently and was sorry for it; for, though I would probably have been cheated in the price, yet I should not have

37

been the cause of injustice and oppression. I had said to the sub-prefect, a few days before, that I wanted the means of transportation for some baggage to Chanchamayo, which he promised to provide for me. Yesterday I went to ask for it, whereupon he referred me to the governor of the district, who was present and who told me that he would have what I required—viz., two asses and a saddle mule, with two peons—ready by to-morrow morning. Accordingly, this morning he sent for me and presented to me the owner of the mule, the owner of the asses, and the two peons. The wages of these were to be four reals, or half a dollar, a day, and I paid each three dollars in advance. To the governor I paid a dollar for each ass and two for the mule, with the understanding that I was to pay as much more on my return. The peons were then lectured on their duties and sent round to my house with an escort of half a dozen *alguaziles,* or constables, armed with sticks, to prevent their escaping or getting drunk before the start. The asses and mules were also sent round under a similar guard, so that my patio seemed filled with a clamorous multitude who created such a confusion that I had to turn out all but my own people. I ordered these to load up, but they said that the owners of the asses had sent no *lassos,* or thongs, to bind on the burdens, and I soon discovered that there was a general unwillingness for the job and that the governor had pressed the animals into the service against the will of the owners.

Strong efforts were made to get the mule away from me. The woman of the house, who, it appears, was a sister of the owner, advised me not to take it; she said that it was a bad, vicious animal that would certainly do me a mischief. I was surprised at this, as he looked particularly docile. I directed my new servant (one recommended by the Cura, and who looked twice as vicious as the mule) to mount and ride him around the patio. The fellow grinned maliciously and proved my judgment correct. Finding that this would not do, the owner (who had put his sister up to making this attempt) then came forward and said I must pay him half a dollar more, as the governor had kept back that much

38

of the price. This being "no go," he tried to steal away his mule while our backs were turned. Being prevented, he went off, got drunk in about fifteen minutes, and came back maudlin; embracing, kissing, and weeping over his mule, crying in piteous tones, *"Mi macho, mi macho"* (my mule, my mule). We shoved him aside and rode off, followed, I have no doubt, by the curses of the community. This was all very annoying to me. I afterwards mentioned these circumstances to the commandant of the fort at Chanchamayo, telling him how much I would prefer to pay double price and get voluntary service.

We got off at noon, stopping at the chacra of General Otero, who gave us a letter to the commandant of the fort of San Ramon. When the old gentleman saw our new servant, whose name is Mariano, he crossed himself most devoutly and ejaculated *"Satanas!"* He then told us that this was a notoriously bad boy, whom nobody had been able to manage, but that we, being strangers and military men, might get along with him by strictness and severity, and he gave the boy a lecture upon his duties and the faithful performance of them.

A mile and a half beyond General Otero's is the town of Acobamba, containing about twelve hundred inhabitants, and six miles further along is a place called Palca, with a population of less than a thousand. We merely passed through, and a mile further on "brought up" at the chacra of Don Justo Rojas, to whom I had a letter from the administrator at Morococha. Don Justo supplied us with a capital supper of chicken soup and boiled eggs, with alfalfa for the beasts. He also sold us, from his establishment in town, sugar and bread. We pitched the tent in an old corn-field and slept delightfully. Tent-pegs for this country should be of iron. Although those we used were made of the hardest wood that could be found in Lima, we had used them all up by this time, beating off their heads by driving them with a hatchet into the hard and stony ground.

Don Justo's is the last chacra in the valley, which now narrows and allows no room for cultivation. Though apparently going down hill, we were evidently crossing a chain of mountains, which the stream at the bottom of the valley has saved us the trouble of ascending and descending, by cleaving a way through for itself and leaving the mountains on either hand towering thousands of feet above our heads. The ride was the wildest we have yet had. The ascents and descents were nearly precipitous, and the scene was rugged, wild, and grand beyond description.

At one place on the road we met with a considerable fright. We were riding in single file along one of its many narrow ascents, where the road is cut out of the mountain side, and the traveller has a perpendicular wall on one hand and a sheer precipice of many hundreds of feet upon the other. Gibbon was riding ahead. Just as he was about to turn a sharp bend of the road, the head of a bull peered round it, on the descent. When the bull came in full view, he stopped. We could see the heads of other cattle clustering over his quarters and hear the shouts of the cattledrivers, far behind, urging on their herd. I happened to be abreast of a slight natural excavation, or hollow, in the mountain side. Dismounting, I put my shoulder against my mule's flank and pressed her into this friendly retreat, but I saw no escape for Gibbon, who had passed it. The bull, with lowered horns and savage, sullen look, came slowly on, and actually got his head between the perpendicular rock and the neck of Gibbon's mule. I felt a spasm of agony, for I thought my companion's fate was sealed. But the sagacious beast on which he was mounted, pressing her haunches hard against the wall, gathered her feet close under her and turned as upon a pivot. This placed the bull on the outside (there was room to pass, though I did not believe it), and he rushed by at the gallop, followed in single file by the rest of the herd. I cannot describe the relief I experienced. Gibbon, who is as gallant and fearless as man can be, said, "It is of no use to attempt to disguise the fact—I was badly scared."

June 18. This was the longest and hardest day's ride. The road was very bad; rocky and rough where it descended the river, steep and difficult where it ascended the mountain side. We thought that the engineer who planned and constructed the road had deliberately selected the worst place to run his road over and that he would have done much better had he occasionally thrown a bridge across the stream and laid out the road along the flank of the mountains on the other side. In seven and a half miles we arrived at *Utcuyacu* (Cotton Water), the first hacienda where we saw sugar-cane, yucca, pine-apples, and plantains.

The road, by which we had descended the valley of Chanchamayo, turned at this place sharp to the right and faced the mountains that divide this valley from that of the Rio Seco. We were near the junction of the two valleys, but a rock had fallen from the hills above and blocked up the road on which we were travelling, so that we had to cross the mountain on our right and get into the other valley. The ascent was steep, trying to man and beast. It is called the *Cuesta de Tangachuca,* or Hill of Take Care of Your Hat, and is about three miles in length. The road, after passing through a thick forest, brought us out upon a bald eminence, the termination of the spur of the Andes that divides the two valleys. The rivers Seco and Chanchamayo unite at its base and flow off through a valley, rapidly widening out, covered with forests and presenting an appearance entirely distinct from the rocky and stern sterility that characterizes the country above.

We descended the hill by a very circuitous and precipitous path, most of us on foot, though it may be ridden over, for Gibbon did ride over the worst parts of it, only dismounting where a fallen tree made an obstruction that he could not pass. The descent brought us to the rocky bed of the Rio Seco, crossing which we were clear of the eastern chain of the Andes and in the Montaña of Chanchamayo. A league from the crossing of the Rio Seco, we passed a broken bridge that spans a small stream coming down a valley from the southward, and halted at the hacienda of Don José Manuel Cardenas, the first of the Montaña, where we camped for the night.

June 19. Six miles of travel brought us to the fort of San Ramon. The road is a black mud bridle-path through the woods,

41

much obstructed with the roots and branches of trees, but level. We were kindly received by the commandant, Don Juan Noel, a fine-looking young man, Captain of Frigate and Lieutenant Colonel in the Army, and his fellow officers.

The fort is a stockade, embracing about six acres, armed with four brass four-pounders and garrisoned with forty-eight men. It is situated at the junction of the rivers Chanchamayo and Tulumayo—the former about thirty and the latter forty yards wide—both shallow and obstructed with rocks. The current seemed about five or six miles the hour. A canoe, well managed, might shoot down the Tulumayo as far as we saw it.

The fort was constructed in 1847 for the purpose of affording protection to the cultivators of the farms in its rear. It doubtless does this against the unwarlike Indians of this country; but I imagine that North American Indians, actuated by feelings of hostility, would cross the rivers above the fort and sweep the plantations before the soldiers could reach them. The Indians have abandoned all idea of reconquering the territory they have lost, but are determined to dispute the passage of the rivers and any attempt at further conquest. They never show themselves now in person, but make their presence evident by occasionally setting fire to the woods and grass on the hill-sides and discharging their arrows at any incautious person who may wander too near the banks of the rivers.

Noel told us that many attempts had been made to establish friendly relations with them. In former times the Indians used to advance out of the forest, to the further bank of the river, and hold conversations and exchange presents with the officers of the post. They gave bows and arrows, rare birds and animals, and received knives, beads, and looking-glasses in return. But these parleys now always ended with expressions of defiance and insult towards the whites on the part of the Indians, and frequently with a flight of arrows. These arrow-shots are of frequent occurrence; several of the soldiers of the fort recently have been severely wounded. A number of arrows were discharged at

42

some soldiers, who were washing their clothes near the banks of the river, while we were here. We picked them up and the commandant made us a present of them.

These arrows, as are the arrows of all the Indians I have met with, are so heavy that, at a greater distance than twenty or thirty yards, it is necessary to discharge them at an elevation, so that they shall describe a curve in the air. It is wonderful to see with what precision the Indians will calculate the arc and regulate the force so that the arrow shall fall upon the target. On the Amazon many fish and turtle are taken with bows and arrows. An Indian in a canoe discharges his arrow in the air. It describes a parabola and lights upon the back of a fish, which the unpractised eye has not been able to see. The barb, with which the arrow is armed, slips on the end of it and is held in its place by a cord which wraps around the shaft of the arrow, tied to its middle. The plunge of the fish shakes the arrow clear of the barb; the cord unwinds, and the arrow floats upon the water—an impediment to the fish and a guide to the fisherman, who follows his arrow till the fish or turtle is dead. The motion of the arrow is so slow, and so readily seen in its course, that I imagine there would be no danger in the reception of single arrow-shots in front, for an abundance of time is allowed to step aside and avoid them. I have seen boys shooting at buzzards on the beach and watched the arrow alight upon the very spot where the bird had been sitting, some seconds after he had left it.

June 23. We started on the return to Tarma, accompanied by the commandant and his servant. We walked up a part of the hill at Tio Seco. This is very hard work. I could not stand it more than half way and made the mule carry me over the rest.

June 24. Missing my saddle-bags, which had some money in them, we sent Mariano (our Tarma servant), accompanied by the servant of the commandant, back to a place some distance the other side of the big hill, where the saddle-bags had been taken off to adjust the saddle. He started at six; we at eight, following our return track. We made the longest and hardest day's ride we

43

had yet made, and were much surprised at being joined by the servants with the saddle-bags at nine P.M. They must have travelled at least thirty-six miles over these terrible roads, crossing the big hill twice and ascending quite two thousand feet. Gibbon did not believe it. He thought—and with much probability—that the boy had hid the saddle-bags at Utcuyacu, and after we left there had produced them and followed in our track, persuading or bribing the soldier to keep the secret. The commandant, however, thought his servant incorruptible and that this was no great feat for these people.

June 26. Discharged Mariano because we could not trust him. Though clever and active, he is neglectful and dishonest. We thought it rather hard that the Cura should have recommended him to us, as his character was notorious in the town. We believed that the Cura, with the people generally, was glad to get rid of him and disposed to palm him off on anybody.

CHAPTER IV

Division of the Party—Acobamba—Plain of Junin—Preservation of Potatoes—Cerro Pasco—Observations

* * *

June 30. Back in Tarma, Gibbon and I have been having long and earnest consultations about the propriety of dividing the party. This I have now decided to do, assigning him the task of exploring the Bolivian tributaries, while I took the headwaters and main trunk of the Amazon. It was a bold, almost a rash determination, for the party seemed small enough as it was, and we might readily encounter difficulties on our route which would require our united exertions to overcome. I had many misgivings and told Gibbon at first that it seemed midsummer madness. However, the prospect of covering such an extent of territory and of being enabled to give an account of countries and rivers so little known, was so tempting that it overrode all objections, and we set about making our preparations for the separation.

We divided our equipment, the tocuyo, or cotton cloth (which we had not yet touched), the hatchets, the knives, the beads, the mirrors, the arms and ammunition. I gave Gibbon fifteen hundred dollars in money, and all the instruments, except some thermometers and the boiling-point apparatus, because I was to travel a route over which sextants and chronometers had been already carried, and he might go where these had never been. I directed him to hire a guide in Tarma, and, so soon as Richards (who was still sick) should be able to travel, to start for Cuzco, and search for the headwaters of the Madre de Dios.

July 1. I started at noon with Ijurra and Mauricio, accompanied

45

by Gibbon and Captain Noel. At General Otero's gate, Noel left us. A very pleasant gentleman this; I shall long remember his kindness. Soon after, Gibbon and I lingered behind the company, and at the entrance of the valley of the Acobamba, which route I was to take, we shook hands and parted. I had deliberated long and painfully on the propriety of this separation. I felt that I was exposing him to unknown perils, and I knew that I was depriving myself of a pleasant companion and a most efficient auxiliary. My manhood, under the depressing influence of these feelings, fairly gave way, and I felt again that swelling of the heart and filling of the eyes that I have so often been called upon to endure in parting from my friends and comrades.

Gibbon returned to make the necessary arrangements of his expedition. We crossed the Chanchamayo by a stone bridge and passed through the village of Acobamba. This town contains about fifteen hundred or two thousand inhabitants, but, like all the towns in the Sierra at this season, it appears deserted—no one in the streets and most of the doors closed.

Six miles further brought us to Palcamayo, a village of one thousand inhabitants. A justice of the peace, a good-looking Indian whom we encountered sitting at the door of a grog-shop in the plaza, conducted us to the house of the alcalde. We found this worthy drunk, asleep on the floor, and were much annoyed with the attentions of another individual, who had a very dirty poultice on his jaws. This was his worship's secretary, who was in little better condition than his patron. Two drunken *regidores* came in to see us, and it seemed that all the magistracy of Palcamayo had been "on a spree." They required the money of us before they would get us or our animals anything to eat.

July 2. Thermometer, at 6 A.M., 37; clear and calm. Three or four miles above Palcamayo the road turns sharp to the westward and ascends a steep and rugged *cuesta*. This brought us out upon a small plain, bounded by low hills and dotted with small detached houses, built of stone and covered with conical roofs of straw. They were circular and looked like bee-hives. The plain

46

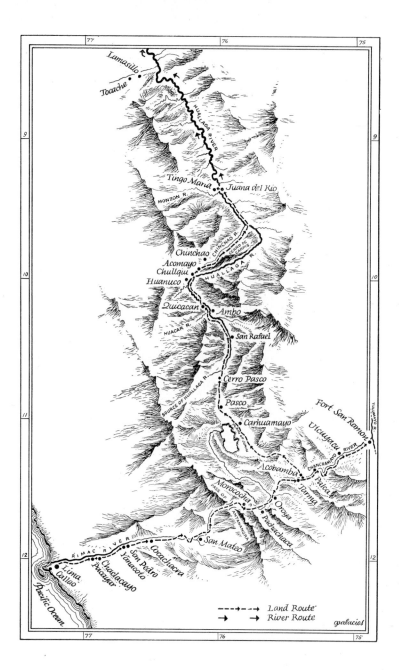

Land Route
River Route

palacios

was covered with a short grass; many tolerable-looking cattle and sheep were feeding on it.

At the western edge of the plain is the village of Cacas, of two hundred and fifty or three hundred inhabitants. The people were celebrating the festival of St. Peter, for they are not particular about days. The church was lighted and decorated with all the frippery that could be mustered, and preparations were making for a great procession. There were two Indians, or Mestizos, dressed in some old-fashioned infantry uniform, with epaulets, flaming red sashes tied in monstrous bows behind, and white gloves. (The cocked hats, for size and variegated plumage, beggar description.) These were evidently the military part of the procession. One was mounted on a little shaggy nag, with his sword hanging on the right-hand side, and the other was strutting about, nearly buried in his cocked hat, while just fourteen men were employed in caparisoning his horse. The drinking had already commenced. Most of the population were getting drunk fast and I have no doubt there was a grand row that night.

July 3. Junin, some eighteen miles from Cacas, is a village of one thousand inhabitants, situated about a mile and a half from the southern extremity of the lake Chinchaycocha and twelve thousand nine hundred and forty-seven feet above the level of the sea. This lake is twenty miles long and is said to discharge its waters into the Amazon by the river of Jauxa, which we crossed at Oroya, and which is a tributary of the Ucayali.

The inhabitants of Junin, like those of the other towns of this plain, are herdsmen. They raise cattle for the supply of Cerro Pasco and Tarma and mules for beasts of burden. Their houses are built of mud and straw, and they eat mutton and *macas* (a root of the potato kind, but looking, and when boiled tasting, more like a turnip). The people of these regions find it very difficult to procure vegetables, as quinua and barley will not grain, nor potatoes grow, in the wet soil and cold atmosphere of the plain. They therefore have to resort to means for preserving the potato and its varieties, which are got from the valleys of the Andes.

49

These means are, generally, drying and freezing; they make a variety of preparations from the potato in this way. The macas are simply exposed to the frost and sun for a number of days, and then put away in a dry room. The inhabitants make a sort of soup or sirup of them, the smell of which, Rivero says, "is a little disagreeable to people unaccustomed to it" (it is really very offensive), and it is the general opinion that it is a stimulant to reproduction.

The plain, about forty-five miles long and from six to twelve broad, is generally wet, and in some places marshy. A great number of large, beautiful waterfowl, including the scarlet flamingo and several varieties of snipe, frequent the banks of the lake and marshy places. The people cut their supply of fuel from the turf of the bogs and stack it up for use in the rainy season. The plain is about thirteen thousand feet above the level of the sea.

The road onward from Junin runs not far from the banks of the lake. On the left we had the grand snow-covered domes and pinnacles of the western Cordillera sleeping in the sunlight, while clouds and storm enveloped the eastern one. About 2 P.M., a breeze from the northward brought some of the storm down upon us. It snowed fast. The flakes were small and round like hail, but soft and white. About fifteen miles from Junin we passed the village of Carhuamayo. Here I saw the only really pretty face I have met within the Sierra and bought a glass of *pisco* from it.

July 4. The village of Ninaccaca, of two or three hundred inhabitants, lies off to the right of the road, on which the local tambo is situated, about half a mile. I would have gone on to the village but I was desirous of sleeping in a tambo, for the purpose of testing the accounts of other travellers who complain so bitterly of them. We were fortunate enough to have the tambo to ourselves, there being no other travellers; and I had quite as comfortable a time as in the alcalde's house at Palcamayo, or in that of the governor of Junin. My bed is generally made on the baggage in the middle of the floor, while Ijurra takes to the standing bed-places, or bunks, which are built of mud and are to be found in every house. Last night I woke up, and finding him very uneasy, I asked him if he had fleas up there. He replied, with the utmost *sang-froid* and as if he were discussing some abstract philosophical question, "This country is too cold for fleas, but this bed-place is crawling with lice." It made my blood run cold; but long before I got out of the Amazon I was effectually cured of fastidiousness upon this or any similar subject.

We were somewhat annoyed by the attentions of the master of the house, who was very drunk. His wife told us next morning that he came near killing her with his knife and would infallibly have beaten her, but that she told him, "Those strangers were soldiers and would shoot him if he did." Her naïve way of telling how she managed the man and got off from the beating was quite amusing. The accent of these people is a sort of sliding drawl that makes every voice alike. They use an imperfect Quichna or Inca language, which I am told is only spoken perfectly in the neighborhood of Cuzco.

Our route now approached the western Cordillera fast. About three miles from the tambo the plain began to be broken into rolling hills. The direction of the road, which had been W.N.W., changed to N.W. by N., and crossed them. After crossing a range, we stopped to breakfast at a collection of a few huts. The Viuda pass of the Cordillera, which is generally crossed by travellers between Lima and Cerro Pasco, was in view from this place.* Immediately after starting, we began passing haciendas for the grinding of ores and getting out silver. They are situated on small streams that come from either the eastern or western Cordillera. They all seem dry at this season, and none of the haciendas are at work. Passed the old village of Pasco. This was once the great mining station, but, since the discovery of the mines at the Cerro, it is falling into decay. The passage of a low but abrupt chain of

* The name Cerro Pasco, or, more properly Cerro de Pasco, is that of a "knot" of mountains uniting the two great ranges (Cordilleras) of the Andes. *H.B.*

51

hills brings the traveller in view of Cerro Pasco. The view from this point is a most extraordinary one. I can compare it to nothing so fitly as the looking from the broken and rugged edges of a volcano into the crater beneath. The traveller sees small houses, built, without regard to regularity, on small hills, with mounds of earth and deep cavities in their very midst; mud chimneys of ancient furnaces, contrasting strikingly with the funnel of the modern steam engine; the huge cross erected on the hill of St. Catalina, near the middle of the city; two beautiful little lakes, only divided by a wide causeway at the southern extremity of the crater, surrounded by hills of five hundred feet in height, with bold white heads of rock; and the magnificent Cordillera from the right and left overlooking the whole.

These are the objects that strike the eye of the traveller at his first view. As he rides down the hill, he sees the earth open everywhere with the mouths of mines now abandoned. He is astonished at their number and feels a sense of insecurity, as if the whole might cave in at once and bury him alive. He rides into the narrow, ill-paved streets of the city, and, if he can divert his attention for a moment from the watching of his horse's footsteps, he will observe the motliest population to be met with anywhere out of the dominions of the Sultan. I believe that he may see, in a single ride through the city, men of all nations, and of almost every condition.

I was delighted when we turned into the patio of the house of the sub-prefect of the province, Don José Mier y Teran, and escaped the rude stare and drunken impertinence of the Indians thronging the streets and the doors of the grog-shops. This gentleman, whose kindness we had experienced at Tarma, gave us quarters in his house and pressed us to make ourselves at home, to which his blunt, abrupt, and evidently sincere manners particularly invited.

After a wash, to which the coldness of the weather and the water by no means invited, I put on my uniform and went out to see Mr. Jump, director of the machinery, and Mr. Fletcher, an em-

ploye of the *Gremio* (Board of Miners), to whom I brought letters
of introduction from Lima. These gentlemen received me with
great cordiality. Mr. Jump offered me a room in his house, and
Mr. Fletcher handed me a number of letters from friends at
home, at Lima, and at Santiago. These letters were cordial medicines to me. I had arrived cold, sick, and dispirited, and but for
them should have passed the first night of mental and physical
suffering that I had been called upon to endure since leaving Lima.

July 6. Rain nearly all night. I was cold and sick and sat by
the fire all day trying to keep myself warm. The houses in Cerro
Pasco are generally built of stones and mud, and covered in with
tiles or straw; most of them have grates, with mud chimneys,
and are plentifully supplied with good coal, both bituminous and
hard. I found very little comfort in them. The houses are so open
about the doors and windows that while my toes were burning my
back was freezing; one has to be constantly twisting round, like
a roasting turkey, to get anything of their benefit. My companion
Ijurra, whose fore-fathers were rich miners and powerful men
in these parts, had many visitors. The talk of the company was of
nothing but the mines, and incessant was the complaining (which
I have heard elsewhere) of the miseries and uncertainties of the
miner's life. All seem to agree that it is a sort of gambling in
which most lose; but there is the same sort of feverish infatuation
in it that there is in gaming with cards, and the unlucky player
cannot but persevere, in the hope that the luck will change and
that the *boya* (striking the rich vein) will come at last.

I went out with Mr. Jump to look at the town. It was a most
curious-looking place, entirely honey-combed, and having the
mouths of mines (some two or three yards in diameter) gaping
everywhere. From the top of the hill called Santa Catalina, the
best view is obtained of the whole. Vast pits, called *Tajos,* surround this hill, from which many millions of silver have been
taken; and the miners are still burrowing, like so many rabbits,
in their bottoms and sides. The hill of Santa Catalina is penetrated in every direction. I should not be surprised if it were to

53

cave in any day and bury many in its ruins. The falling in of mines is of frequent occurrence. Only four days ago a mine fell in and buried five; four have been recovered, but one is still incarcerated, and the people are now hard at work for him.

July 8. Visited the mines. We entered a mouth which seemed only a little larger than that of a common well, each of the party furnished with a tallow candle, fixed in an iron contrivance at the end of a staff. The descent was disagreeable, and, to the tyro, seemed dangerous. The earth was moist, and the steps merely holes dug for the heels at irregular distances. I feared every moment that my boot-heel would slip, and was heartily glad when we got upon the apparently level and broad bank of the great *socabon,* having made up my mind that I would tempt Providence no more. But, reflecting that I should probably never visit the mines of Cerro Pasco again, I took courage and descended one hundred and ten feet further, by an even worse descent than the former, to the bottom of the pump shafts. A burly and muscular Cornishman, whom I at first took to be a Yankee, with a bit of candle stuck into a lump of mud in front of his hat, was superintending here, growling at the laziness and inefficiency of his Indian subordinates. I should think that these pumps were not well attended to, so far from the eye of the master. They are worked by chains and long copper rods. All the metal work of the pumps is of copper. Iron is corroded very quickly, on account of the sulphuric acid and sulphates which the water of the mines holds in solution. The fish are said to have abandoned the lake of Quiulacocha, into which the waters are forced, on this account. The sides of the mines were covered in many places with beautiful sulphates of iron and copper. Our exploration lasted about four hours. We emerged at the tajo of Sta. Rosa, where, seated upon piles of silver ore, we partook of some bread and cheese and a glass of pisco, which we found as welcome and as grateful as manna in the desert.

July 9. As a consequence of yesterday's excursion, I am suffering to-day from an affection called *macolca,* which is incident to

54

MINER, CERRO PASCO

nearly every one on his first visit to the mines. This is a painful soreness of the muscles, particularly on the front of the thigh. I could scarcely bear that anything should touch my legs, and locomotion was anything but agreeable.

The town of Cerro Pasco is a little more than fourteen thousand feet above the level of the sea. One authority gives it as fourteen thousand two hundred and seventy-nine. The population varies from six to fifteen thousand souls, according to the greater or less yield of the mines. Most of the adult part of this population are, of course, engaged in mining. There are no ladies—at least I saw none in society. The men meet to discuss the mines, the probable price of silver, and to slander and abuse each other. There seems to be no religion here, even in form. The churches are mere barns, going to decay, and I saw no processions or religious ceremonies.

The climate of this place is exceedingly uncomfortable, and I should suppose unhealthy. I could not sleep between sheets, but preferred "the woolens," with an abundance of them. In July, August, and September there is a great fall of snow and hail, which lowers the thermometer considerably; even without these it goes down to 30° and 28° in August. From the middle of October to the end of April the climate is insupportable. There is a period of fine weather from the middle of December to the middle of January, called, in the poetic language and religious turn of thought of the Spaniards, *El verano del niño,* or the summer of the child, from its happening about Christmas. The streams, which are fed from the rains of this country, invariably stop rising and fall a little after this period. The temperature is so rigorous here that the hens do not hatch, nor the llamas procreate. Women, at the period of their confinement, are obliged to seek a more genial climate, or their offspring will not live.

July 13. I had unfortunately selected a feast-day, and one, too, on which there was a regular bull fight (the first that had been seen in the Cerro), for my departure, and found great difficulty in getting off. The muleteers I had engaged were drunk at an early

57

hour and I had to send the police after them. It is really curious to observe how entirely indifferent to the fulfilment of a promise these people are, and how very general the vice is. These muleteers had given me the strongest assurances that they would be at my door by daylight, and yet when they made the promise they had not the slightest idea of keeping it. The habit seems to be acquiesced in and borne with patience by even the true and promise-keeping English. My friend Mr. Jump did not sympathize in the least with my fretfulness and seemed surprised that I expected to get off.

CHAPTER V

Departure from Cerro Pasco—San Rafael—Ambo—Quicacan—
Huanuco—Cerro de Carpis—Chinchao Valley—Huallaga River

*   *   *

By cajoling and threats of appeal to the military (a small military
force is stationed here as a police), we got our drunken vagabonds
to "load up" and set off by half-past 1 P.M. One of them gave
us the slip at the outskirts of the town. The other wished to look
him up, or at least to get the key of a tambo where two spare mules
belonging to them were locked up, but we would not hear of it.
The deserter joined us at our stopping-place for the night, but
on finding the condition of things, he had to return to the Cerro
for his missing beasts.

Almost immediately on leaving the Cerro, and ascending the
hills that encircled it on the north, we came in sight of the Eastern
Andes, which is here a cordillera, for it has many abrupt and
snow-clad peaks. Close at hand, on the left, was a spot of marshy
ground, which had some interest for us, as we were not to quit
the waters which we saw trickling in tiny streams from it until,
swelled by many others, they pour themselves into the Atlantic
by a mouth one hundred and eighty miles broad. This is the
source of the Huallaga, one of the head tributaries of the Amazon.

July 14. We had a pleasant ride down the valley, which opens
a little and gives room for some cultivation. There were pinks
and hollyhocks in the little gardens adjoining the cottages; also
cabbages, lettuce, and onions. The rock of this district is red sandstone. We passed a hacienda, where there were roses in bloom and

the flowering pea, with wheat on the hill-side and a grist-mill.
We also saw alfalfa and maize. Gypsum crops out of the hills on
the road-side, making the roads white. Houses here are whitewashed with it. We continually met mules laden with tobacco,
coca, and fruit going to the Cerro. We stopped, at half-past five,
at San Rafael, an Indian town of some two hundred and fifty
souls, with a white lieutenant-governor, and put up at his house.
I had my bed made inside, instead of outside the house, which
was a mistake, as I was "pigging in" with all the family; and
from want of air, and villainous smell, I expected to catch the
fever—if not worse—before morning. The thermometer was at
62° at 7 P.M., and I imagine did not fall lower than 50° during
the night, so that I could very well have slept outside.

July 15. We got alfalfa for our mules, but it is now getting
very scarce. The valley, after leaving San Rafael, is very narrow.
The road rises and falls along the bare flanks of the mountains.
We shot at condors hovering over a dead mule, and saw a small
hawk of variegated and pretty plumage. About ten miles from
San Rafael we were crossing the highest part of the chain. An
opening in the mountains to the right gave us a view of some
splendid snow-clad peaks. After an hour's ride over a precipitous and broken path, rendered dangerous in some places by the
sliding of the earth and soft rock from above upon it, we commenced a very sharp descent, which brought us, in fifteen minutes, to fruit-trees and a patch of sugar cane on the banks of the
stream. The sudden transition from rugged mountain peaks, where
there was no cultivation, to a tropical vegetation was marvellous.
A few miles further on we crossed the boundary-line between the
provinces of Pasco and Huanuco. I was glad to exchange the
mining for the agricultural country. At half-past four we arrived
at the town of Ambo, a village of one thousand inhabitants,
situated at the junction of the rivers Huacar and Huallaga. The
former stream comes down a ravine to the westward. Each is
about thirty-five yards broad, and, uniting, they pour their waters
by the town with great velocity.

Two miles from Ambo, on the right or opposite bank of the river, is another very pretty little village, almost hidden in the luxuriant vegetation about it. The whole valley now becomes very beautiful. The blended green and yellow of the fields of sugar cane and alfalfa, divided by willows, interspersed with fruit-trees, and broken into wavy lines by the serpentine course of the river, presented a gay and cheerful appearance, which, contrasting with the forbidding aspect of the rocks we had just left, indicated that we had exchanged a semi-barbarous for a civilized society. The only drawback with me was excessive fatigue. When I arrived (at five) at the hospitable gates of the hacienda of Quicacan, and with difficulty lifted myself out of the saddle, it was with the deep sigh which always accompanies relief from pain, and which was much more pleasurable than the sight of waving fields and babbling brooks.

The owner of the hacienda—an English gentleman named Dyer to whom I brought letters from Cerro Pasco—received me and my large party exactly as if it were a matter of course and as if I had quite as much right to enter his house as I had to enter an inn. The patio was filled with horses, belonging to a large party from Huanuco bound to Lima, and every seat in the ample portico seemed filled. I was somewhat surprised at the size and appointments of the establishment. It looked like a little village of itself, with its offices and workshops. The dwelling—a large, substantial, though low building, with a corridor in front supported on massive arches, and having the spaces between the pillars enclosed with iron wire to serve for cages for numerous rare and pretty birds—occupied one side of the enclosed square; store-rooms occupied another; the sugar-house, another; and a chapel, the fourth. A bronze fountain, with an ample basin, decorated the centre. I was strongly reminded of the large farm-houses in some parts of Virginia—the same number of servants bustling about in each other's way; the children of the master and the servant all mixed up together; the same hospitable welcome to all comers; the same careless profusion. When I saw the servants dragging out mattresses and bed-clothing from some obscure room, and going with them to different parts of the house to make pallets for the visitors who intended to spend the night, I seemed carried back to my boyish days, and almost fancied that I was at a country wedding in Virginia. We dined at six in another spacious corridor, enclosed with glass, and looking out upon a garden rich with grape-vines and flowers. After dinner, the party broke up into groups for cards or conversation, which continued until ten o'clock brought tea and bed-time.

I conversed with an intelligent and manly Frenchman named Escudero. His account of the seeking and gathering of Peruvian bark was exceedingly interesting, and I should judge that it is an occupation which involves much fatigue and exposure. I also had some talk with quite a pretty young woman, who had come from Quito by the way of the Pastaza, Marañon, and Huallaga rivers. She said she was scared at the *malos pasos,* or rapids of the river, and never could relish monkey soup; but what gave her most uneasiness was the over-eager attentions of the Huambisas Indians. She declared that this was frightful, and swore a good round oath that might well have satisfied Hotspur, *"Caramba!* but they were mad for a white wife.'' Report here says that she prefers Yankee to Indian, and is about to bestow her hand upon a long countryman of ours, the head blacksmith, named Blake.

July 16. Dyer had put me into a wide "four-poster." None but a traveller in these parts can imagine the intense pleasure with which I took off my clothes and stretched my weary limbs between linen sheets and laid my head upon a pillow with a frilled case to it. I could scarcely sleep for the enjoyment of the luxury. Rest, too, has renewed my beast. The little black, which I thought last night was entirely done up, is this morning as lively as a filly.

We left Quicacan at noon, in company with Mr. Dyer and my French friend. We stopped at another hacienda, about a mile and a half from this, belonging to a gentleman named Ingunza, and at another a little lower down, called Andabamba, belonging to

62

Señor San Miguel, to whom I brought letters from Lima. All these, with another on the same road, belonged to a Colonel Lucar, of Huanuco, who gave them to these gentlemen, his sons-in-law. Quicacan was the family mansion, and had been longest under cultivation. At half-past four we arrived at Huanuco, and, presenting a letter to Colonel Lucar from his son-in-law Dyer, we were kindly received and lodgings appointed us in his spacious and commodious house.

July 17. Huanuco, founded in 1539, is one of the most ancient cities in Peru. It is prettily situated on the left bank of the Huallaga river, which is here about forty yards wide and at this time (the dry season) about two feet deep in the channel. A smaller stream, called the Higueros, empties into it just above the city. The houses are built of adobe, with tile roofs, and almost all have large gardens attached to them—so that the city covers a good deal of ground without having many houses. The gardens are filled with vegetables and fruit-trees and make delightful places of recreation during the warmer parts of the day. There are no less than fifteen churches in the city, some of them quite large and handsome. The people are civil and respectful, and, save a curious stare now and then at my spectacles and red beard, are by no means offensive in their curiosity.

The trade of the place is with Cerro Pasco on the one hand and the villages of the Huallaga on the other. It sends chancaca, tobacco, fruit, and vegetables to the Cerro, and receives foreign goods (mostly English) in return. A shop-keeper gave me the price of some of the articles in his store: broad striped cassimere, such as gentlemen's trousers are made of, five and a half dollars the yard; very common silk handkerchiefs, one dollar; common hat, five dollars; blue cloth, twenty-five cents the yard; baize, eighty-seven and a half cents; a narrow ribbon, one dollar and twenty-five cents the piece; cotton handkerchiefs, two dollars and twenty-five cents the dozen; tolerable Scotch carpeting, one dollar and a half the vara, of thirty-three English inches; bayeta castilla (a kind of serge or woolen cloth, with a long shag upon it, and of rich colors), one dollar and seventy-five cents the vara. Vegetables and fruit are abundant and cheap. This is, *par excellence*, the country of the celebrated chirimoya. I have seen this fruit in Huanuco quite twice as large as it is generally seen in Lima, and of most delicious flavor. They have a custom here to cover the finest specimens with gold leaf and place them as a decoration on the altar of some patron Saint on his festival. The church afterwards sells them, and I have seen several on Colonel Lucar's table.

This gentleman is probably the richest and most influential man in Huanuco. He seems to have been the father of husbandry in these parts, and is the very type of the old landed proprietor of Virginia, who has lived always upon his estates and attended personally to their cultivation. Seated at the head of his table, with his hat (which he insisted upon removing unless I would wear mine) on to keep the draught from his head, his chair surrounded by two or three little Negro children, whom he fed with bits from his plate, the meanwhile attending with patience and kindness to the clamorous wants of a pair of splendid peacocks, a couple of small parrots of brilliant and variegated plumage, and a beautiful and delicate monkey—I thought I had rarely seen a more perfect pattern of the patriarch.

I sold my mules to the Colonel for half that I had given for them, with the condition that we should ride them as far as practicable and send them back by the arriero. The old gentleman agreed to it, though rather reluctantly. He said that some fifteen years ago, a countryman of mine, and calling himself an officer of the navy also, had sold him his mules for pistols and fowling-pieces, on the same terms; but when he arrived at the end of his journey, he sold the mules again, and went off with the proceeds. The Colonel could not give me the name of this individual. I afterwards ascertained that he was not an American, but a German.

July 22. Much to my annoyance our servant Mauricio deserted this morning. Ijurra accuses me of having spoiled him by indulgence, and I, on the other hand, think that he had disgusted him by tyranny. I imagine he went back to Lima with a young man named Castillo who was going to the capital with stuffed birds' skins to sell. This was an intelligent young man who gave me information about the Montaña. He said I would be amply protected in my contemplated voyage up the Ucayali with twenty-five Chasutinos (Indians of Chasuta), for they were a brave and hardy people; but that the Cocamas and Cocamillos, from about the mouth of the river, were great cowards, and would desert me on the first appearance of the savages—that they had so treated him. I rather suspect that the reason for Don Mauricio's shabby behavior was that we were getting into his own country and that he had private reasons for desiring to avoid a visit home.

Our arriero made his appearance at noon, instead of early in the morning as he had promised; but we are now getting used to this. We did not ride our own mules, as they were sick and not in condition to travel, and the arriero supplied us with others. I got a horse, but did not derive much benefit from the exchange. We found the road good, but rocky. Six miles from Huanuco we passed the village of Sta. Maria del Valle, of three hundred inhabitants. We stopped and took some fruit and pisco with the curate, to whom I also had a letter from Lima. Every traveller in this country should provide himself with letters of introduction. People, it is true, will receive him without them, but do not use that cordial and welcome manner which is so agreeable.

July 23. Course still N.E. along the banks of the Huallaga. Trees principally small acacias. At six miles from the hacienda of Chullqui we crossed the river, turned to the north, and ascended a ravine (down which flowed a small stream) to the village of Acomayo. The water here is very good, which was an agreeable change from the Huanuco water, and the fruits, oranges, figs, guavas, and chirimoyas, are of good quality. I noticed, also, a tree bearing a large bell-shaped flower, called *floripondo*. This is an old acquaintance of mine. It gives out a delicious fragrance at night, which accompanied, as I have known it, by soft air, rich

65

moonlight, and gentle company makes bare existence a happiness.

About three miles up the "Quebrada" we turned to the north-east and commenced the ascent of the Cerro de Carpis. This is one of a range of mountains running to the southward and eastward. The ascent is six miles long and very tedious. There is said to be a superb view of the Montaña from the summit, but the clouds (almost within reach of the hand) boiling up from the great deep below, effectually cut it off and we could see nothing. When we had got some distance down and obtained a view through an opening in the thick growth of the mountain-side, we looked down upon the most rugged country I have ever seen. There seemed to be no order or regularity in the hills which were thickly covered with forest; but the whole had the appearance of the surface of a vast boiling caldron suddenly stricken motionless. Just at the summit, and where the road turns to descend, hundreds of little wooden crosses were placed in the niches of the rock— votive offerings of the pious arrieros, either of gratitude for dangers passed or for protection against dangers to come in the ascent or descent of the mountain.

July 24. An hour's travel brought us to the bottom of the Cerro de Carpis, and after a ride of seven miles we came to the village of Chinchao, containing twelve houses and a church, with cotton, coffee, orange, and plantain trees scattered about the village. A pretty shrub, bearing a gay, red flower, in appearance like our crêpe myrtle, bordered the road-side. The cultivation of coca commences here.

I brought a letter from the sub-prefect at Huanuco, for the governor of Chinchao, but he was absent and not to be found. We then asked for the lieutenant governor, but though there seemed, from the general account, to be such a person, we could not find out exactly who he was, or where he lived. The arriero said he lived "a little lower down," but at every house at which we called in our descent the reply still was *mas abajo* (yet lower). At last we seemed to have treed him, and even the man's wife was produced; but after a little conversation it appeared that our friend was still *mas abajo*. I was tired and hungry enough to wish he was where he could not get any lower, for we had depended upon our letter for a breakfast. We continued our weary route, and at the next house (the best-looking we had seen) encountered a white woman, rather shrewish-looking, indeed, but still a woman, synonym everywhere for kindness. Ijurra civilly inquired if we could get a few eggs. I think our appearance, particularly the guns slung behind the saddles, bred mistrust, for we met with the invariable lie, *no hay* (haven't got any). I couldn't be baffled in this way. So, taking off my hat and making my best bow, in my most insinuating tones I said, "We have something to eat in our saddle-bags, and would be very much obliged if La Señora would permit us to alight and take our breakfast there." She softened down at once and said that if we had any tea she could give us some nice fresh milk to mix with it. We had no tea, but declared, with many thanks, that the milk would be very acceptable. Whereupon, it was "put on" to boil; and, moreover, a dozen fresh eggs, and boiled to perfection, were also produced. I enjoyed the breakfast very much, and was pluming myself on the effect of my fine address, when (alas for my vanity!) the lady, after looking at my companion for some time, said to him, "Arn't you *un tal* (a certain) Ijurra?" He said yes. "Then we are old playmates," said she. "Don't you recollect our play-ground, your old uncle's garden in Huanuco, and the apples you used to steal out of it to give me? I'm Mercedes Prado." Here was the solution to the enigma of our reception. Strange to say, the name awoke pleasant recollections in me also, and set before me the features of a certain gay and beautiful young girl whose quick repartee and merry laugh added so much to the charm of Valparaiso society.

July 25. The means of living are getting very scarce. We could get nothing to eat today and had to draw upon our small store of provisions. Near night we stopped at Chihuangala, the last hacienda of the valley, and beyond which there is no mule-road. The arrieros left us to seek pasturage. This is our last dealing with this gentry. I was glad to dismount, for I was tired of riding; but in spite of the abuse that is generally heaped upon the arrieros, I think I have had little difficulty to complain of. They seem to be tolerably honest and faithful (when once on the road), and with judicious treatment one can get along with them very comfortably.

July 26. At this place we were to await the Indians from Tingo Maria (a village at the head of canoe navigation on the Huallaga) to carry our luggage on. Ijurra had written from Huanuco to the governor of Tingo Maria, requesting him to send them to us at Chihuangala.

We had hard commons here, our provisions beginning to decay. No eggs; no potatoes; nothing, in fact, but yuccas and bananas. There were turkeys, chickens, and a pig running about, but no entreaty, nor any reasonable offer of money, could induce the people to sell us one. I offered the *patrona* a dollar and a half for a half-grown turkey; but she said she must wait till her husband came in from his work, so that she might consult him. When he came, after long debate, it was decided that they would sell me a chicken for breakfast tomorrow. I tried hard to find out why they were so reluctant to sell, for they do not eat them themselves, but did not succeed. I believe it to be something like the miser-feeling of parting with property, the not being used to money, and also a dislike to kill what they have reared and seen grow up under their own eye.

July 28. I walked, in company with Ijurra, about three miles to visit a Señor Martins, at his hacienda of Cocheros. We found this gentleman a clever and intelligent Portuguese who has passed many years in this country. His wife is Doña Juana del Rio, a very lady-like person, in spite of her common country costume. It was quite surprising to see a Limeña, and one who had evidently lived in the first circles of that city, in this wild country, and in this rude though comfortable house. The floor was earth and I saw no chairs. The lady sat in a hammock, and the men either on the mud benches around the sides of the room or on a coarse wooden one alongside of a clumsy table. Part of the house was curtained off into small bed-rooms. There was evident plenty, and great comparative comfort about the house; also, a fine lot of handsome, intelligent-looking children.

We met, at Cocheros, an English botanist named Nation, upon whose track we have been ever since leaving Lima. He was the gardener of Souza Ferreyra, the Brazilian Chargé in Lima, and I believe was collecting plants for him. Poor fellow, he had had a hard time of it. He lost his mule not long after leaving Lima and had to walk from Surco to Morococha, where some kind person supplied him with another. He has also had tertiana whenever he has gone into the Montaña. He was alone, and spoke no Spanish, but he had combatted obstacles and difficulties with a spirit and perseverance deserving all praise. Mr. Nation, who has sent a great many specimens of plants to Lima, says that the "flora" of this country is almost identical with that of Brazil.

On our return from Cocheros we stopped at the house of a man who had, the day before, promised to sell us a fowl; with the usual want of good faith of these people, he now refused. Ijurra took the gun from my hand, and, before I was aware what he was about to do, shot a turkey. The man and his wife made a great outcry over it, and he was hurrying off, with furious gestures and menacing language, to report the matter to his patron, when a few kind words, the helping myself to a chew of coca out of his *huallqui,* or leathern bag, in which it is carried, and the offer of a dollar and a half, which before he had indignantly spurned, changed his mood. He smiled and expressed himself satisfied, now that the thing was done and it could not be helped. I had been often told by travellers that this was frequently necessary to get something to eat, but had always set my mind resolutely against any such injustice and oppression. I expressed my opinion of the matter to Ijurra and requested that the like should not occur again.

July 30. At 10 A.M., when we had begun to despair of the coming of our Indians, and Ijurra was about to start alone for Tingo

69

Maria, for the purpose of fetching them, they came shouting into the inn yard, thirteen in number. They were young, slight, muscular-looking fellows, all life and energy, and wanted to shoulder the trunks and be off at once. We, however, set them to breakfast. At noon we started and descended the valley of Chinchao. The path was steep and obstructed with bushes.

At about six miles from Chihuangala we arrived at the junction of the Chinchao river with the Huallaga, in a heavy shower of rain, with thunder and lightning. The Huallaga is here some sixty yards wide, and the Chinchao thirty, both much obstructed with shoals and banks of gravel. The peons waded the Huallaga above the junction, and brought up a canoe in which we went down the river to the hacienda of Chinchayvitoc. The Indians managed very well. It was a great treat, after the tedious walk we had had, to feel the free, rapid motion of the boat as it glided down the stream.

Chinchayvitoc is a hacienda for the collection of Peruvian bark established by a Bolivian gentleman named Villamil. He brought some Bolivians with him to search for the bark, but it is not to be found in this country of good quality and the scheme seems a failure. There is a mayordomo and a family of Indians living at the hacienda, but it looks empty and deserted.

We had Mr. Nation with us. He had collected some valuable plants and showed me one which he said was a present for an Emperor and that its very name would make my journal famous. I of course did not ask it of him, but was very glad to be able to repay to him, in some slight measure, the many kindnesses I have received from his countrymen by giving him a part of my bedclothes and making him comfortable for the night, which he seemed to be much in need of, for he was wet and sick.

We met at this place some Indians carrying tobacco from Tocache and Saposoa (towns of the Huallaga) to Huanuco. Enterprising men have frequently tried to establish a trade along this river, carrying down cotton goods, knives, hatchets, beads, &c., and getting return cargoes of tobacco, rice, straw hats, rare birds,

70

and animals, but the difficulties of the route seem to have baffled enterprise. About two and a half years ago a man named Vicente Cevallos made a large venture. He carried down thirty-five trunks or packages of goods, and the people of the river still talk of his articles of luxury; but in passing one of the *malos pasos,* or rapids of the river, his boat capsized, and he lost everything.

July 31. I bathed in the river before starting. This is wrong in so humid an atmosphere. I became chilled and did not get over it for some hours. A native traveller in these parts will not even wash his face and hands before the sun is well up. At half-past 4 P.M., we arrived at "The Cave," a place where a huge rock, projecting from the hill-side, made a shelter which would cover and protect from dew or rain about a dozen persons. The Indian who carried my bag of bedding wished to make my bed there, but I decided that it was too damp and made him spread it out on the shingle by the river bank. A tin pan of hot boiled rice flavored with cheese, a teacup of brandy, and half a dozen cigars made us very comfortable. Lulled by the rustling of the leaves and the roar of the river, we slept in spite of the ants and other insects that left the mark of their bites upon our carcasses. I saw here, for the first time, the *luciernago,* or fire-fly of this country. It is, unlike ours, a species of beetle, carrying two white lights in its eyes (or, rather, in the places where the eyes of insects generally are) and a red light between the scales of the belly, so that it reminded me something of the ocean steamers. It has the power of softening the light of the eyes until it becomes very faint; but upon irritating it, by passing the finger over the eyes, the light becomes very bright and sparkling. They are sometimes carried to Lima (enclosed in an apartment cut into a sugar-cane), where the ladies, at balls or theatres, put them in their hair for ornament.

August 1. We started, without breakfast, at a quarter to seven, thinking that we were near Tingo Maria. But it was ten miles distant, and I was weary enough ere we arrived. My principal source of annoyance was the having inadvertently asked how far we were from our destination. I would advise no traveller to do this; he is sure to be disappointed. The Indians take no account of time or distance. They stop when they get tired and arrive when God pleases. They live on plantains—roasted, boiled, and fried. In the way of food, a yucca is their greatest good. Talking with a young Indian who had a light load and kept up with me very well, I was struck with the comparative value of things. A Londoner, who has been absent for some time from his favorite city and subjected to some privations on that account, could not have spoken of the elegances and comforts of London with more enthusiasm than my companion spoke of Pueblo Viejo, a settlement of half a dozen Indians, which we were approaching. "There are plantains," said he; "there are yuccas; there is everything" (*Hay platanos; hay yuccas; hay todo*), and I really expected to be surprised and pleased when I arrived at Pueblo Viejo. The town, in fact, consisted of a single hut, with a plantain grove, a small patch of yuccas, and another of sugar-cane.

At eleven we arrived at Juana del Rio, a settlement of five or six houses, on the right bank of the river. The houses were all shut up and nobody seemed to be at home. Here we crossed the river (one hundred yards broad, smooth, and deep), and walked down the left bank about half a mile to the pueblo of San Antonio del Tingo Maria. *Tingo* is the Indian term for the junction of two rivers, the Monzon emptying into the Huallaga just above this. The governor, an intelligent and modest young man, a former friend of Ijurra, welcomed us cordially and gave us a capital breakfast of chicken broth.

CHAPTER VI

Tingo Maria—Vampires—Blow-guns—Canoe Navigation—Shooting Monkeys—Tocache—Sion—Salt Hills of Pilluana

*   *   *

August 2. Tingo Maria is a prettily-situated village, of forty-eight able-bodied men, and an entire population of one hundred and eighty-eight. This includes those who are settled at Juana del Rio and the houses within a mile or two.

The pueblo is situated in a plain on the left bank of the river, which is about six miles in length and three miles in its broadest part, where the mountains back of it recede in a semi-circle from the river. The height above the level of the sea is two thousand two hundred and sixty feet. The productions of the plain are sugar-cane, rice, cotton, tobacco, indigo, maize, sweet potatoes, yuccas, and *sachapapa* (potato of the woods), the large, mealy, purple-streaked tuberous root of a vine, in taste like a yam, and very good food. The woods are stocked with game such as *pumas*, or American tigers; deer; peccary, or wild hog; *ronsoco*, or river hog; monkeys, &c. For birds there are several varieties of *curassow*, a large bird, something like a turkey, but with, generally, a red bill, a crest, and shining blue-black plumage; a delicate *pava del monte*, or wild turkey; a great variety of parrots; large, black, wild ducks; and cormorants. There are also rattlesnakes and vipers. But even with all these, I would advise no traveller to trust to his gun for support. The woods are so thick and tangled with undergrowth that no one but an Indian can penetrate them, and no eyes but those of an Indian could see the game. Even he only hunts from necessity and will rarely venture into the thick forest alone, for fear of the tiger and the viper. There are also good and delicate fish in the river, but in no great abundance.

Ijurra shot a large bat, of the vampire species, measuring about two feet across the extended wings. This is a very disgusting-looking animal, though its fur is very delicate and of a glossy, rich maroon color. Its mouth is amply provided with teeth, looking like that of a miniature tiger. I never heard it doubted, until my return home, that these animals were blood-suckers; but the distinguished naturalist Mr. T. R. Peale tells me that no one has ever seen them engaged in the operation and that he has made repeated attempts for that purpose, but without success. Never having heard this doubt, it did not occur to me to ask the Indians if they had ever seen the bat sucking, or to examine the wounds of the horses that I had seen bleeding from this supposed cause.

I saw here, for the first time, the blow-gun of the Indians, called, by the Spaniards, *cerbatana;* by the Portuguese of the river, *gravatana* (a corruption, I imagine, of the former, as I find no such Portuguese word) ; and by the Indians, *pucuna.* It is made of any long, straight piece of wood, generally of a species of palm called chonta—a heavy, elastic wood, of which bows, clubs, and spears are also made. The pole or staff, about eight feet in length and two inches diameter near the mouth end, tapering down to half an inch at the extremity, is divided longitudinally ; a canal is hollowed out along the centre of each part, which is well smoothed and polished by rubbing with fine sand and wood. The two parts are then brought together, nicely wound with twine, and the whole covered with wax, mixed with some resin of the forest to make it hard. A couple of boar's teeth are fitted on each side of the mouth end, and one of the curved front teeth of a small animal resembling a cross between a squirrel and a hare is placed on top for a sight. The arrow is made of any light wood, generally the wild cane, or the middle fibre of a species of palm-leaf, which is about a foot in length and of the thickness of an ordinary match. The end of the arrow, which is placed next to the mouth, is wrapped with a light, delicate sort of wild cotton which grows in

74

a pod upon a large tree and is called *huimba*. The other end, very sharply pointed, is dipped in a vegetable poison prepared from the juice of the creeper, called *bejuco de ambihuasca,* mixed with *aji,* or strong red pepper, *barbasco, sarnango,* and whatever substances the Indians know to be deleterious.

The marksman, when using his pucuna, instead of stretching out the left hand along the body of the tube, places it to his mouth by grasping it, with both hands together, close to the mouthpiece, in such a manner that it requires considerable strength in the arms to hold it out at all, much less steadily. If a practised marksman, he will kill a small bird at thirty or forty paces. In an experiment that I saw, the Indian held the pucuna horizontally and the arrow blown from it stuck in the ground at thirty-eight paces. Commonly the Indian has quite an affection for his gun and many superstitious notions about it. I could not persuade one to shoot a very pretty black-and-yellow bird for me because it was a carrion bird; the Indian said that it would deteriorate and make useless all the poison in his gourd. Neither will he discharge his pucuna at a snake, for fear of the gun being made crooked like the reptile, and a fowling-piece or rifle that has once been discharged at an alligator is considered entirely worthless. A round gourd, with a hole in it for the huimba, and a joint of the *caña brava* as a quiver, completes the hunting apparatus.

August 3. Went to church. The congregation—men, women, and children—numbered about fifty. The service was conducted by the governor, assisted by the alcalde. A little naked, bow-legged Indian child, of two or three years, and Ijurra's pointer puppy, which he had brought all the way from Lima on his saddlebow, worried the congregation with their tricks and gambols; but altogether they were attentive to their prayers, and devout. I enjoyed exceedingly the public worship of God with these simple people of the forest; and, although they probably understood little of what they were about, I thought I could see its humanizing and fraternizing effect upon all.

At night we had a ball at the governor's house. The alcalde, who was a trump, produced his fiddle. Another had a rude sort of guitar, or banjo. Under the excitement of the music we danced till eleven o'clock. The *Señor Commandante* was in considerable request, and a fat old lady, who would not dance with anybody else, nearly killed me. The governor discharged our guns several times and let off some rockets that we had brought from Huanuco. I doubt if Tingo Maria had ever witnessed such a brilliant affair before.

August 4. I waked up with pain in the legs and headache from dancing, and found our men and canoes ready for embarkation. After breakfast the governor and his wife (though I grievously fear that there had been no intervention of the priest in the matter of the union), together with several of our partners of the previous night, accompanied us to the port. After loading the canoes, the governor made a short address to the canoe-men, telling them that they were to take good care of us; whereupon, after a glass all round, from a bottle brought down specially by our hostess, and a hearty embrace from the governor, his lady, and my fat friend of the night before, we embarked and shoved off, the boatmen blowing their horns as we drifted rapidly down with the current of the river, and the party on shore waving their hats and shouting their adieus.

We had two canoes, the largest about forty feet long by two and a half feet broad. Each was hollowed out from a single log, and manned by five men and a boy. They are conducted by a *puntero,* or bowman, who looks out for rocks or sunken trees ahead; a *popero,* or steersman, who stands on a little platform at the stern of the boat and guides her motions; and the *bogas,* or rowers, who stand up to paddle, having one foot in the bottom of the boat and the other on the gunwale. When the river was smooth and free from obstructions, we drifted with the current, the men sitting on the trunks and boxes, chatting and laughing with each other; but, as we approached a mal-paso, their serious looks and the firm position in which each one planted himself at his post showed that work was to be done. I felt a little nervous at first, but when we had fairly entered the pass, the rapid gesture of the puntero, indicating the channel; the elegant and graceful position of the popero, giving the boat a broad sheer with the sweep of his long paddle; the desperate exertions of the bogas; the railroad rush of the canoe; and the wild, triumphant, screaming laugh of the Indians, as we shot past the danger, made a scene that was much too exciting to admit of any other emotion than that of admiration.

At half-past five we camped on the beach. The first business of the boatmen when the canoe is secured is to go off to the woods and cut stakes and palm branches to make a house for the *patron*. By sticking long poles in the sand, chopping them half in two, about five feet above the ground, and bending the upper parts together, they make, in a few minutes, the frame of a little shanty, which, thickly thatched with palm leaves, will keep off the dew or an ordinary rain. Some bring the drift-wood that is lying about the beach and make a fire; the provisions are cooked and eaten; the bedding laid down upon the leaves that cover the floor of the shanty; the mosquito nettings spread; and, after a cup of coffee, a glass of grog, and a cigar (if they are to be had), everybody retires for the night by eight o'clock. The Indians sleep around the hut, each under his narrow cotton mosquito curtain, and the curtains glisten in the moon-light like so many tomb-stones.

August 5. Started at eight. River seventy yards broad, nine feet deep, pebbly bottom; current three miles per hour. We find in some places, where hills come down to the river, as much as thirty feet of depth. I was surprised that we saw no animals all day, but only river birds, such as ducks, cormorants, and king-fishers. We also saw many parrots of various kinds and brilliant plumage, but they always kept out of shot. We camped at half-past five, tired and low-spirited, having had nothing to eat all day but a little rice boiled with cheese early in the morning. My wrists were sore and painful from sunburn, and the sand-flies were very troublesome.

August 6. Soon after starting we saw a fine doe coming down

77

towards the river. We steered in and got within about eighty yards of her, when Ijurra and I fired together, the guns loaded with a couple of rifle-balls each. The animal stood quite still for a few minutes, and then walked slowly off towards the bushes. I gave my gun, loaded with three rifle-balls, to the puntero, who got a close shot, but without effect. One of the balls, a little flattened, was picked up close to where the deer stood. These circumstances made the Indians doubt if she were a deer; and I judged from their gestures and exclamations, that they thought it was some evil spirit that was ball-proof.

These Indians have very keen senses and see and hear things that are inaudible and invisible to us. Our canoe-men this morning commenced paddling with great vigor. When I asked the cause, they said that they heard monkeys ahead. I think we must have paddled a mile before I heard the sound they spoke of. When we came up to them, we found a gang of large red monkeys in some tall trees on the river-side, making a noise like the grunting of a herd of enraged hogs. We landed, and in a few minutes I found myself beating my way through the thick undergrowth and hunting monkeys with as much excitement as ever I had hunted squirrels when a boy. I had no balls with me, and my No. 3 shot only served to sting them from their elevated position in the tops of the trees, and bring them within reach of the pucunas of the Indians. They got two and I one, after firing about a dozen shots into him. I never saw animals so tenacious of life; this one was, as the Indians expressed it, *bathed in shot* (*banado en municion*). These monkeys, about the size of a common terrier, were clad with a long, soft, maroon-colored hair. I believe they are of the species commonly called "howling monkeys."

When I arrived at the beach with my game, I found that the Indians had made a fire and were roasting theirs. They did not take the trouble to skin and clean the animal, but simply put him in the fire, and, when well scorched, took him off and cut pieces from the fleshy parts with a knife. If these were not sufficiently well done, they roasted them farther on little stakes stuck up be-

78

fore the fire. I tried to eat a piece, but it was so tough that my teeth would make no impression upon it.

We also saw to-day several river hogs and had an animated chase after one, which we encountered on the river-side, immediately opposite a nearly precipitous bank of loose earth, which crumbled under his feet so that he could not climb it. He hesitated to take the water in face of the canoes, so that we thought we had him; but after a little play, up and down the river-side, he broke his way through the line of his adversaries, capsizing two Indians as he went, and took to the water. This animal is amphibious, about the size of a half-grown hog. It reminded me, in its appearance and movements, of the rhinoceros. It is also red, and I thought it remarkable that the only animals we had seen—the deer, the monkeys, and the hog—should be all of this color.

We found the river to-day much choked with islands, shoals, and grounded drift-wood; camped at half-past five, and supped upon monkey soup. The monkey, as it regards toughness, was monkey still; but the liver, of which I ate nearly the whole, was tender and good. Jocko, however, had his revenge, for I nearly perished of nightmare. Some devil, with arms as nervous as the monkey's, had me by the throat, and, staring on me with his cold, cruel eye, expressed his determination to hold on to the death. I thought it hard to die by the grasp of this fiend on the banks of the strange river, and so early in my course. Upon making a desperate effort and shaking him off, I found that I had forgotten to take off my cravat, which was choking me within an inch of my life.

August 7. To-day presented a remarkable contrast to yesterday for sportsmen. We saw not a single animal, and very few birds; even parrots, generally so plentiful, were scarce to-day. It was a day of work. The men paddled well and we must have made seventy miles. On approaching Tocache, which was their last stage with us, the Indians almost deafened me with the noise of their horns. These horns are generally made of pieces of wood hollowed out thin, joined together, wrapped with twine, and

79

coated with wax. They are shaped like a blunderbuss and are about four feet long; the mouthpiece is of reed, and the sound deep and mellow. The Indians always make a great noise on approaching any place to indicate that they come as friends. They fancy that they might otherwise be attacked, as hostile parties always move silently.

We arrived at five. Wearied with the monotonous day's journey and the heat of the sun, I anticipated the arrival with pleasure, thinking that we were going to stop at a large village and get something good to eat, but I was grievously disappointed. We arrived only at the port,* which was, as usual, a shed on a hill. The village itself was nine miles off. There was nothing to eat where we were, so we determined to start inland and see what we could pick up. A rapid walk of an hour and a quarter brought us to Lamasillo, which I had been told was a pueblo of whites, but which we found to be but a single house. I had been under the impression that "pueblo" meant a village, but I think now it signifies any settled country, though the houses may be miles apart. With much persuasion we induced the people of the house to sell us a couple of bottles of aguadiente and a pair of chickens. We were given to understand that Tocache was two *coceadas* further on, or about the same distance that we had come over from the port to this place. Distance is frequently estimated by the time that a man will occupy in taking a chew of coca. From the distance between the port and Lamasillo, it appears that a chew of coca is about three-fourths of a league, or thirty-seven and a half minutes.

We walked back by moonlight and had a fowl cooked forthwith. As we had had nothing but a little monkey soup early in the morning, we devoured it more like tigers than Christian men. We made our beds in the canoes under the shed, and, tired as we were, slept comfortably enough. It seems a merciful dispensation

* As used here, and throughout the rest of Herndon's narrative, the word "port" should be read as "river landing." *H.B.*

of Providence that the sand-flies go to bed at the same time with the people; otherwise I think one could not live in this country.

August 8. I sent Ijurra to Tocache to communicate with the governor, while I spent the day in writing up my journal and drying the equipage that had been wetted in the journey. In the afternoon I walked into the woods with an Indian, for the purpose of seeing him kill a bird or animal with his blow-gun. I admired the stealthy and noiseless manner with which he moved through the woods, occasionally casting a wondering and reproachful glance at me as I would catch my foot in a creeper and pitch into the bushes with sufficient noise to alarm all the game within a mile round. At last he pointed out to me a toucan, called by the Spaniards *predicador,* or preacher, sitting on a branch of a tree out of the reach of his gun. I fired and brought him down with a broken wing. The Indian started into the bushes after him, but, finding him running, he came back to me for his blow-gun, which he had left behind. In a few minutes he brought the bird to me with an arrow sticking in its throat. The bird was dead in two minutes after I saw it, and probably in two and a half minutes from the time it was struck. The Indian said that his poison was good, but that it was in a manner ejected by the flow of blood, which covered the bird's breast, and which showed that a large blood-vessel of the neck had been pierced. I do not know if his reasoning was good or not.

Ijurra returned at eight, tired and in a bad humor. He reported that he had hunted the governor from place to place all day; had come up with him at last and obtained the promise that we should have canoes and men to prosecute our journey. My companion, who has been sub-prefect or governor of the whole province which we are now in (Mainas) and who has appointed and removed these governors of districts at pleasure, finds it difficult to sue where he had formerly commanded. He consequently generally quarrels with those in authority, and I have to put myself to some trouble to reconcile the difference and cool

81

down the heats which his impatience and irritability often occasion. He, however, did good service to the cause, by purchasing a hog and some chickens.

August 9. We had people to work killing and salting our hog. We had difficulty in getting some one to undertake this office, but the man from whom we purchased the hog brought down his family from Lamasillo to do the needful. We had very little benefit from our experiment in this way. We paid eight dollars for the hog, twenty-five cents for salt, twenty-five cents to Don Isidro, who brought him down to the port, and fifty cents to the same gentleman for butchering him.

Everybody is a Don in this country. Our Indian boatmen, at least the poperos, are Dons. Much ceremonious courtesy is necessary in intercourse with them. I have to treat the governors of the districts with all manner of ceremony. At the same time, while they exact this, and will get sulky and afford me no facilities without it, every last one of them will entertain the proposition to go along with me as my servant.

August 10. Whilst bathing in the river, I saw an animal swimming down the stream towards me, which I took to be a fox or cat. I threw stones at it and it swam to the other side of the river and took to the forest. Very soon after, a dog, who was evidently in chase, came swimming down, and missing the chase from the river, swam round in circles for some minutes before giving up. This animal, from my description, was pronounced to be an ounce, or tiger-cat. It is called *tigre* throughout all this country, but is never so large or ferocious as the Indian tiger. They are rather spotted like the leopard, than striped like the tiger. They are said, when hungry, to be sufficiently dangerous, and no one cares to bring them to bay without good dogs and a good gun. We talked so much about tigers and their carrying off people while asleep, that I, after going to bed, became nervous, and every sound near the shed made me grasp the handles of my pistols.

August 12. Had a visit from the governor last night. He is a little, bare-footed Mestizo, dressed in the short frock and trousers

82

of the Indians. He seemed disposed to do all in his power to facilitate us and forward us on our journey. I asked him about the tigers. He said he had known three instances of their having attacked men in the night; two of them were much injured, and one died.

Our boatmen made their appearance at 10 A.M., accompanied by their wives. The women carry their children (lashed flat on the back to a frame of reeds) by a strap around the brow as they do any other burden. The Indians of this district are Ibitos. They are less civilized than the Cholones of the Tingo Maria, and are the first whose faces I have seen regularly painted. They seem to have no fixed pattern but each man paints according to his fancy; using, however, only two colors, blue and red.

We started at twelve with two canoes and twelve men. River fifty yards broad, eighteen feet deep, and with three miles an hour current; a stream called the Tocache empties into it about half a mile below the port. It forces its way through five channels, over a bank of stones and sand. The river is now entirely broken up by islands and rapids. In passing one of these, we came very near being capsized. Rounding suddenly the lower end of an island, we met the full force of the current from the other side, which, striking us on the beam, nearly rolled the canoe over. The men, in their fright, threw themselves on the upper gunwale of the boat which gave us a *heel* the other way, and we very nearly filled. Had the popero fallen from his post (and he tottered fearfully), we should probably have been lost; but by great exertions he got the boat's head down stream, and we shot safely by the rocks that threatened destruction.

At six we arrived at the port of Balsayacu. The pueblo, which I found, as usual, to consist of one house, was a pleasant walk of half a mile from the port. We slept there instead of at the beach, and it was well that we did, for it rained heavily all night. The only inhabitants of the rancho seemed to be two little girls, but I found in the morning that one of them had an infant, though she did not appear to be more than twelve or thirteen years of age.

I suppose there are more houses in the neighborhood; but, as I have before said, a pueblo is merely a settlement and may extend over leagues. We travelled to-day about twenty-five miles.

August 13. Last night Ijurra struck with a fire-brand one of the boatmen, who was drunk and disposed to be insolent, and blackened and burned his face. The man—a powerful Indian, of full six feet in height—bore it like a corrected child in a blubbering and sulky sort of manner.

Between ten and eleven we passed the mal-paso of Matagalla, just below the mouth of the river of the same name, which comes in on the left, clear and cool into the Huallaga. This mal-paso is the worst that I have yet encountered. We dared not attempt it under oar. The canoe was let down along the shore, stern foremost, by a rope from its bows, and guided between the rocks by the popero—sometimes with his paddle, and sometimes overboard, up to his middle in water.

At 1 P.M. we arrived at the port of Sion. This is the port *de la madre,* or of the main river. There is another port situated on the caño, or arm of the main river, nearer the pueblo. The village lies about a mile from the port. As our Tocache men were to leave us here, we had all the baggage taken up to the town. The walk is a pleasant one, over a level road of fine sand, well shaded with large trees. Ijurra, who went up before me, met the priest of Saposoa (who is on the annual visit to his parish) going south, and about to embark at the caño port; and the governor of the district going north to Pachiza, the capital. This last left orders that we should be well received, and the lieutenant-governor of the pueblo lodged us in the *convento,* or priest's house, and appointed us a cook and a servant.

I slept comfortably on the padre's bedstead, enclosed with matting to keep off the bats. The people appear to make much of the visit of their priest. I saw in the corner of the *sala,* or hall of the house, a sort of rude palanquin, which I understood to have been constructed to carry his reverence back and forth between the city and port.

August 14. We employed the morning in cleaning the arms and drying the equipage. Had a visit from some ladies, pretty Mestizas (descendants of white and Indian), who examined the contents of our open trunks with curiosity and delight. They refrained, however, from asking for anything until they saw some sugar with which we were about to sweeten our morning coffee. They could then contain themselves no longer, and requested a bit. This seems an article of great request, for no sooner had the news spread that we had it, than the alcalde brought us an egg to exchange for some. Even the lieutenant-governor expressed his desire for a little. We refused the dignitaries, though we had given some to the ladies, for we had but enough for two or three cups more. Their wants, however, were not confined to sugar. After a while they asked, without scruple, for anything they saw. The lieutenant-governor wanted a little sewing cotton, and some of the soap we brought to wash ourselves with to take for physic. These things we could more easily part with, and I had no objection to giving him some, and also regaled his wife with a pair of pinchbeck earrings. There is nothing made or cultivated here for sale. The people raise a few fowls and some yuccas and plantains for their own use; and it was well that we brought our own provisions along, or we might have starved. The whole town and neighborhood, reckoning women and children, is three hundred.

The town appears to have been once in a better condition than it is now. There are remains of a garden attached to the convent, and also of instruments of husbandry and manufacture—such as rude mortars, hollowed out from the trunk of a tree, for beating (with pestles) the husk from rice, and a press for putting into shape the crude wax gathered from the hollow trees by the Indians, used by the friars "lang syne"—all now seem going to decay. The people are lazy and indifferent. They cultivate plantains sufficient to give them to eat, and yuccas enough to make masato to get drunk on. This seems all they need. Most of their time is spent in sleeping, drinking, and dancing. Yesterday they were dancing all day, having a feast preparatory to going to work to clear ground for our "Lady of Something."

The dance was a simple affair so far as figure was concerned —the women whirling round in the centre, and the men (who were also the musicians) trotting around them in a circle. The music was made by rude drums and fifes of reed, and it was quite amusing to see the alcalde, a large, painted, grave-looking Indian, trotting round like a dog on a tread mill, with a penny whistle in his mouth. I myself have heard their music—the last thing at night as I was going to bed, and the first thing in the morning as I was getting up—for days at a time. The tune never changes, and seems to be the same everywhere in the Montaña. It is a monotonous tapping of the drum, very like our naval *beat to quarters.*

We embarked at the caño port, and dropped down the caño a mile and a half to the river. We found the river deep and winding, and running, generally, between high cliffs of a white rock. The white, however, is superficial, and seems to be imparted by age and weather. We passed the mal-paso of Shapiama, and, with fifteen minutes' interval, those of Savolayacu and Cachihua-nushca. In the first two the canoes were let down with ropes, and we shot the last under oar, which I was surprised at, as I had heard that it was one of the worst on the river.

About sunset we arrived at Challuayacu, a settlement of twenty houses. All the inhabitants, except those of one house, were absent. We were told that they had been disobedient in some matter to the governor of the district and that he had come upon them with a force and carried them off prisoners to Juan Juy, a large town further down the river, where authority might be brought to bear upon them. The village is situated in a large and fertile plain, but this is not yet settled or cultivated, and, as at Sion, nothing is produced except the bare necessaries of life.

August 16. Lovely morning. On stepping out of the house my attention was attracted by a spider's web covering the whole of a large lemon-tree nearly. The tree was oval and well shaped, and the web was thrown over it in the most artful manner, with the finest effect. Broad flat cords were stretched out like the cords of a tent from its circumference to the neighboring bushes, and it looked as if some genius of the lamp, at the command of its master, had exhausted taste and skill to cover with this delicate drapery the rich-looking fruit beneath. I think the web would have measured full ten yards in diameter.

At noon we arrived at the mouth of the Huayabamba, which is one hundred yards wide, has six feet of water, and a beautiful pebbly bottom. A quarter of an hour's drag of the canoe along the right bank brought us to the village of Lupuna, the port of Pachiza. It contains fifteen houses and about seventy-five inhabitants. A little rice is grown, but the staple production is cotton, which seemed to be abundant. This may be called a manufacturing place, for almost every woman was engaged in spinning, and many balls of cotton thread were hanging from the rafters of each house. A woman, spinning with diligence all day, will make four of these balls. These weigh a pound and are worth twenty-five cents. They are very generally used as currency, there being little money in the country.

We had a visit from the governor of Pachiza, a town situated on the right bank of the river three miles above Lupuna. I asked him why he had carried away prisoners nearly all the population of Challuayacu. He merely said that they had been rebellious and resisted his authority, and therefore he had taken them to Juan Juy where they could be secured and punished.

After we had retired to our mats beneath the shed for the night, I asked the governor if he knew a bird called *El alma perdida*. He did not know it by that name and requested a description. I whistled an imitation of its notes, whereupon an old crone, stretched on a mat near us, commenced, with animated tones and gestures, a story in the Inca language, which, translated, ran somehow thus:

87

An Indian and his wife went out from the village to work their chacra, carrying their infant with them. The woman went to the spring to get water, leaving the man in charge of the child, with many cautions to take good care of it. When she arrived at the spring, she found it dried up and went further to look for another. The husband, alarmed at her long absence, left the child and went in search. When they returned, the child was gone, and to their repeated cries, as they wandered through the woods in search, they could get no response save the wailing cry of this little bird, heard for the first time, whose notes their anxious and excited imagination "syllabled" into *pa-pa, ma-ma* (the present Quichua name of the bird). I suppose the Spaniards heard this story, and, with that religious, poetic turn of thought which seems peculiar to this people, called the bird "the lost soul."

The circumstances under which the story was told—the beautiful, still, starlight night—the deep, dark forest around—the faint-red glimmering of the fire, flickering upon the old woman's gray hair and earnest face as she poured forth the guttural tones of the language of a people now passed away—gave it a sufficiently romantic interest to an imaginative man. The old woman was a small romance in herself. I had looked at her with interest as she cooked our supper. She wore a costume that is sometimes, though not often, seen in this country. The body, or upper part of the dress, which was black, consisted of two parts—one coming up from the waist behind and covering the back; the other in front, covering the breast; and the two tied together over each shoulder with strings, leaving her lank sides and long skinny arms perfectly bare.

August 17. We procured a canoe sufficiently large to carry all our baggage (we had hitherto had two), with eight peons. We found hills now on both sides of the river, which a little below Lupuna has one hundred and twenty yards of breadth and thirty feet of depth. We passed a small raft, with a house built of cane and palm upon it, containing an image of the Virgin, which was bound up the river seeking contributions. The people buy a step towards Heaven in this way with their little balls of cotton.

We passed abreast of Juan Juy, but, a long island intervening, we did not see it. It is a large village of five hundred inhabitants, situated in a plain, a great part of which is overflowed by the river at full stage. Much rice is cultivated there. We stopped at a collection of three or four huts called Oge, where there was a trapiche to grind sugar-cane, but the people only made bad rum of it. We tried to purchase yuccas and plantains. Though they had them, they did not care to sell. Below this we passed a rancho on the right-hand side, where there was a fine field of maize. This is the first settlement we have seen on that bank. Fear of the savages, or *Infidels*, as they are called, who dwell on that side, prevent it.

We stopped for the night at Juan Comas, a small village situated on a bluff of light sandy soil on the left bank. The hills on the other side are much more bare than is common, having only a few small trees and scattering bushes on them. We were quite objects of curiosity, and most of the people of the village came in to see us. One man, a strapping fellow, came in, and after a brief but courteous salutation to me, turned to one of the women and drove her out of the house with kicks and curses. He followed her and I soon after heard the sound of blows and the cries of a woman. I suppose the fellow was either jealous, or the lady had neglected some household duty to gratify her curiosity.

August 18. This part of the river is called the "well" of Juan Comas. It is half a mile in length and the current runs but one and a quarter mile the hour. The hills terminate just below this and we have the country flat on both sides. Soon after we passed the mouth of the river Hunanza, a small stream coming in on the Infidel side of the river. Our popero says that the Infidels dwell near here, and the people of Tarapoto go a short distance up this river to capture the young Indians and take them home as slaves. I believe this story, for I found servants of this class in Tarapoto, who were bought and sold as slaves. Slavery is prohibited by the laws of Peru, but this system is tolerated on the plea that the Infidel is Christianized and his condition bettered by it.

The hills of Pilluana, which we now soon passed, have their base immediately upon the river on the right-hand side. They are about three hundred feet in height and stretch along the banks of the river for a quarter of a mile. The salt, for which they are famous, shows like frost upon the red earth at a distance; but seen nearer, the heavy rains seem to have washed away the loose earth and left nearly the pure salt standing in innumerable cone-shaped pinnacles, so that the broken sides of the hills look like the crater of a volcano or the bottom of a geyser. Where the hills have been excavated, beautiful stalactites of perfectly pure salt hang from the roof in many varieties of shapes. There are much higher hills back of these which appear also to contain salt, so that there seems enough of a supply here for all people and all time.

We passed the mouth of the river Mayo, which comes in on the left between moderately high hills, and five minutes after arrived at Shapaja, one of the ports of Tarapoto. Shapaja has twenty houses, mostly concealed in the high groves of plantains which surround them. Nearly all the men were away fishing, but the women (as always) received us kindly and cooked our supper for us.

CHAPTER VII

*Tarapoto—Chasuta—Yurimaguas—Santa Cruz—Antonio—La-
guna—Mouth of the Huallaga*

*   *   *

August 19. We started in company with a man who, with his
peons, was carrying fish that he had taken and salted below
Chasuta to Tarapoto. A smart walk of five hours (the latter part
of it very quick, to avoid the rain that threatened us) brought us
to the town. The road crossed a range of hills in the forest for
about half the distance. The ascent and descent of these hills
were tedious, because light showers of rain had moistened the
surface of the hard-baked earth and made it as slippery as soap.
For the other half of the distance the road ran over a plain covered with high, reedy grass and some bushes; there was a short
clump-grass underneath that would afford capital pasturage.
The distance between Shapaja and Tarapoto I judge to be fifteen miles, and the direction westerly, although I could not tell
exactly, on account of the winding of the road.

Tarapoto—which is situated upon a moderate eminence near
the western edge of the plain before spoken of and surrounded by
hills, which are mountains in the west—is by far the largest town
I have seen since leaving Huanuco. The district—comprising
the towns of Tarapoto, Chasuta, Cumbasa, Morales, Shapaja,
Juan Guerra, and Juan Comas—numbers six thousand inhabitants.

The principal productions are rice, cotton, and tobacco, all
of which are articles of export, particularly the cloth called
gocuyo, woven by the women from cotton. Nearly all the course of

91

the river, as far as Egas, is supplied from Tarapoto with this article. It also goes inland as far as Moyobamba, where it is exchanged for straw hats and English prints.

There is little or no money in this country. Tocuyo, wax from the Ucayali, and balls of cotton thread are used in its place. The English goods that come from the interior sell in Tarapoto for four times their cost in Lima. I suppose there is a little money obtained for these articles in Huanuco and Chachapoyas, or left here by travelling strangers. But if so, it falls into the hands of the traders and is hoarded away. These traders are either Moyobambinos (inhabitants of Moyobamba) or foreigners of Spain, France, and Portugal. The Moyobambinos will compass sea and land to make a dollar. I met with them everywhere on the river, and I think that I did not enter an Indian village without finding a Moyobambino domiciliated and trading with the inhabitants. They are a thin, spare, sickly-looking people, of a very dark complexion, but seem capable of undergoing great hardship and fatigue, for they carry their cargoes of goods hundreds of leagues distant by roads and rivers that present innumerable difficulties.

They bear a bad character on the river and are said to cheat and oppress the Indians; so that when I could not get a yucca for my supper without paying for it in advance, I vented my spleen by abusing a Moyobambino who had treated the people so badly that they distrusted everybody. But I have had reason, once or twice, for abusing other people besides Moyobambinos on this account. The governor of Tarapoto hesitated about trusting me with a canoe to descend the river, because a person representing himself as a countryman of mine had run off with one some years before.

I met at this place my countryman Hacket, whom I had heard spoken so highly of in Cerro Pasco and Huanuco. He is employed in making copper kettles (called *pailas*) for distilling and in all kinds of blacksmith and foundry work. He seems settled in this country for life, and has adopted the habits and manners of

92

the people. Poor fellow—how rejoiced he was to see the face and hear the speech of a countryman!

The people have no idea of comfort in their domestic relations. The houses are of mud, thatched with palm, and have uneven dirt floors. The furniture consists of a grass hammock, a standing bed-place, a coarse table, and a stool or two. The governor of this populous district wore no shoes and appeared to live pretty much like the rest of them.

An American circus company passed through Tarapoto a few months ago. They had come from the Pacific coast and were bound down the Amazon. This beats the Moyobambinos for determined energy in making dollars. I imagine that the adventure did not pay, for I encountered traces of them, in broken-down horses, at several of the villages on the river. They floated their horses down on rafts.

August 21. We started for Juan Guerra on horseback in company with a large fishing-party, got up by the padre for his own profit. He seemed to carry nearly the whole town with him. The mounted party consisted of eight. There were two ladies along, whose company added to the gaiety and pleasure of the canter through the woods. Used as I had become by my travels in various parts of the world to the free and easy, I must confess that I was a little startled to see these ladies, when we arrived at Juan Guerra, denude themselves to a silk handkerchief around the loins and bathe in the river in full sight of all the men.

Arrived at Juan Guerra, we embarked upon the Cumbasa, which empties into the Mayo. The fishing-party of the padre was a large affair. They had four or five canoes and a large quantity of barbasco. The manner of fishing is to close up the mouth of a caño of the river with a net-work made of reeds, and then, mashing the barbasco root to a pulp, throw it into the water. This turns the water white, and poisons it, so that the fish soon commence rising to the surface dead, and are taken into the canoes with small tridents. Almost at the moment of throwing the barbasco into the water, the smaller fish rise to the surface and die

93

in two or three minutes; the larger fish survive longer. A successful fishing expedition of this sort is a matter of half a day, or till the canoes are filled.

August 22. Chasuta, where we now are, is the port of the district of Tarapoto. The traders have their cargoes carried on the backs of Indians between Tarapoto and Chasuta, and embark and disembark at the latter place to avoid the rapids of the Pongo. There were canoes in the port, just arrived from below, with salt fish and wax, and others about to start down with the products of the district. The salt fish brought up from below is in large pieces of about eight pounds each, cut from the *vaca marina;* the *payshi,* a fish of one hundred and fifty pounds weight; and the *gamitana,* a large flat fish, like the skate.

The *vaca marina* (sea cow) of the Spaniards, and *peixe boy* (fish ox) of the Portuguese (also found in our Florida streams and there called *manatee*), is found in great numbers on the Amazon and its principal tributaries. It is an animal averaging, when full grown, about nine feet in length and six in circumference. It has much the appearance of a large seal, with a smooth skin, dark on the back, a dirty white on the belly, and thinly sprinkled with coarse hairs. The eyes and ears (or rather holes for hearing) are very small. The mouth is also small, though it looks large on the outside, on account of a very thick and wide upper lip, which is shaped like that of an ox. In the one I examined, which was a young female, I could discover neither tongue nor teeth, but a thick, rough, and hard fleshy cushion attached to both upper and lower jaws, which seemed to me very well adapted to masticating the grass which grows upon the banks of the river, and which is its principal food. The tail is broad and flat and is placed horizontally. This, with two large fins far in advance, and very near the jaws, enables it to move in the water with considerable rapidity. It is not able to leave the water; in feeding it gets near the shore and raises its head out. It is, when feeding, most often taken by the Indians. An ordinary-sized vaca marina will yield from thirty-five to forty pounds of manteca, which will sell for three cents the pound, besides ten pieces of salt fish, worth twelve and a half cents each. The governor general of the missions told me that two men in his employment on the Amazon had taken seven for him in eight days. The flesh, salted or dried, is a good substitute for pork. It is put up in large jars in its own fat and is called *michira*.

Chasuta is an Indian village of twelve hundred inhabitants, situated on a plain elevated about twenty-five feet above the present level of the river. It is frequently covered in flood-stage, and the people take their canoes into their houses and live in them. The Indians of Chasuta are a gentle, quiet race. They are tolerably good boatmen, but excel as hunters. Like all the Indians, they are much addicted to drink. I have noticed that the Indians of this country are reluctant to shed blood and seem to have a horror of its sight. I have known them to turn away to avoid killing a chicken, when it was presented to one of them for that purpose. The Indian whom Ijurra struck did not complain of the pain of the blow, but, bitterly and repeatedly, that "his blood had been shed." They eat the mosquitoes that they catch on their bodies, with the idea of restoring the blood which the insect has abstracted.

The padre told me that the fee for a marriage was four pounds of wax, which was the perquisite of the sacristan; for a burial, two, which went to the sexton; and that he was regaled with a fowl for a christening. I bought wax of the curate to pay for the canoes and boatmen. The men desired money, and I told the curate that he had better let me pay them in money, as to be familiar with its use would tend to civilize them. But he said that they did not know its value and would only hoard it up or use it as ornaments. I was tempted to believe him, for certainly it never circulates. I have not seen a dollar since I left Huanuco except those that were in my own hands.

As we were now clear of the dangers of the river and were to be more exposed to sun and rain, we had coverings made of hooppoles and thatched with palm fitted to the canoe. The one over the stern, for the accommodation of the patron, covers about six feet of it and makes a good den to retreat to in bad weather. It is called by the Indians *pamacari*. The one fitted over the cargo, in the body of the boat, is called *armayari*. It is narrower than the other, allowing room for the Indians to sit and paddle on each side of it.

August 25. We left Chasuta in company with two canoes: one belonging to a Portuguese, resident of Tarapoto, carrying a cargo to Nauta; and the other carrying the padre's little venture of salt. We passed the salt hills of Callana Yacu, where the people of Chasuta and the Indians of Ucayali and Marañon get their salt. The hills are not so high as those of Pilluana and the salt seems more mixed with red earth. It "crops out" on the banks of the river, which rise into gentle hills as they recede, covered with bushes and small trees. A quarter of an hour afterwards we entered a more hilly country; river narrow, shallow, and rapid; its depth fifteen feet and its current four and a half miles the hour. Soon after we passed between the cliffs of dark-red rocks, where the river deepened to forty-two feet. On one of these rocks, appearing like a gigantic boulder of porphyry, were cut rude figures of saints and crosses, with letters which are said to express "The Leap of the Traitor Aguirre"; but they were too much worn by time and weather for me to make them out. There were more recent cuttings in the rock. I noticed the letters VR—the work, I imagine, of somebody belonging to the circus company. The pass is called El Salto de Aguirre.

August 26. Being in company with Antonio, the Portuguese, who knows how to arrange matters, we get a cup of coffee at the peep of day and are off by half-past 5 A.M. At five miles of distance we passed the lower extremity of the Pongo, which commences at Shapaja. *Pongo* is an Indian word and is applied to designate the place where a river breaks through a range of hills, and where navigation is of course obstructed by rocks and rapids. The place where the Marañon breaks its way through the last chain of hills that obstructs its course is called the Pongo de Man-seriche. This is the Pongo de Chasuta.

After passing the Pongo, we entered upon a low, flat country, where the river spreads out very wide and is obstructed by islands and sandbanks. This is the deposit from the Pongo. Small pebbly islands are forming in the river and much driftwood from above lodges on them. After having stopped two hours to breakfast, we passed the mouth of the Chipurana, which is about twenty yards wide.

August 27. Saw flesh-colored porpoises; also a small seal, which looked like a fur-seal; got turtle-eggs. The turtles crawl out upon the beach during the night, deposit their eggs, and retreat before dawn, leaving, however, broad tracks in the sand, by which their eggs are discovered. We must have got upwards of a thousand. I counted one hundred and fifty taken from one hole. Since we have passed the Pongo, we have encountered no stones; the beaches are all of sand.

August 28. Arrived at Yurimaguas. This little village, situated upon a hill immediately upon the banks of the river and numbering two hundred and fifty inhabitants, now appears almost entirely deserted. We could procure neither peons nor canoes. The men were away in the forest collecting wax for a fiesta, and the sub-prefect of the province, who had been gold-hunting up the Santiago, had taken all the canoes. I was told that his expedition for gold up the Santiago, which consisted of a force of eighty armed men, had been a failure; that they got no gold, and had lost five of their company by the attacks of the savages. We could buy nothing at Yurimaguas but a few bunches of plantains and some salt fish out of a passing boat. We left there after breakfast.

We met several canoes going up the river for salt; canoes passing each other on the river *speak* at a great distance apart. The Indians use a sing-song tone that is heard and understood very far, without seeming to call for much exertion of the voice. Every year at this season the Indians of the Marañon and Ucayali make

97

a voyage up the Huallaga for their supply of salt. They travel slowly and support themselves by hunting, fishing, and robbing plantain patches on their way.

We tried an experiment to ascertain the speed of the canoe at full oar, and I was surprised to find that six men could not paddle it faster than two miles the hour. Ours, however, is a very heavy and clumsy canoe. We have had frequent races with Antonio and the padre, and were always beaten. It was a pretty sight to see the boat of the latter, though laden with salt to the water's edge, dance by us; and, although beaten, we could not sometimes refrain (as their puntero, a tall, painted Indian, would toss his paddle in the air with a triumphant gesture as he passed) from giving a *hurrah* for the servants of the church.

August 29. We met a canoe of Conibos Indians, one man and two women, from the Ucayali, going up for salt. We bought (with beads) some turtle-eggs, and proposed to buy a monkey they had; but one of the women clasped the little beast in her arms, and set up a great outcry lest the man should sell it. The man wore a long, brown, cotton gown, with a hole in the neck for the head to go through and short, wide sleeves. He had on his arm a bracelet of monkey's teeth, and the women had white beads hanging from the *septum* of the nose. Their dress was a cotton petticoat tied round the waist.

We are now getting into the lake country. From this region to the mouth of the Amazon, lakes of various sizes, and at irregular distances, border the rivers. They all communicate with the rivers by channels which are commonly dry in the dry season. They are the resort of immense numbers of water-fowl, particularly cranes and cormorants. The Indians, at the proper season, take many fish and turtles from them.

Many of these lakes, according to the traditions of the Indians, are guarded by an immense serpent which is able to raise such a tempest in the lake as to swamp their canoes, whereupon it immediately swallows the people. It is called in the "Lengua Inga" *Yacu Mama,* or mother of the waters. The Indians never enter a

ZAPARO

Wagner & McGuigan's Lith Phila.

lake with which they are not familiar that they do not set up an obstreperous clamor with their horns, which the snake is said to answer, thus giving them warning of its presence.

I never saw the animal myself, but will give a description of it written by Father Manuel Castrucci de Vernazza, in an account of his mission to the *Givaros* and *Zaparos* of the river *Pastaza*, made in 1845:

"The wonderful nature of this animal—its figure, its size, and other circumstances—enchains attention, and causes man to reflect upon the majestic and infinite power and wisdom of the Supreme Creator. The sight alone of this monster confounds, intimidates, and infuses respect into the heart of the boldest man. He never seeks or follows the victims upon which he feeds; but, so great is the force of his inspiration, that he draws in with his breath whatever quadruped or bird may pass him, within from twenty to fifty yards of distance, according to its size. That which I killed from my canoe upon the Pastaza (with five shots of a fowling-piece) had two yards of thickness and fifteen yards of length; but the Indians of this region have assured me that there are animals of this kind here of three or four yards diameter, and from thirty to forty long. These swallow entire hogs, stags, tigers, and men, with the greatest facility; but, by the mercy of Providence, it moves and turns itself very slowly, on account of its extreme weight. When moving, it appears a thick log of wood covered with scales, and dragged slowly along the ground, leaving a track so large that men may see it at a distance and avoid its dangerous ambush."

It is almost impossible to doubt a story told with this minuteness of detail. Doubtless the padre met with, and killed a boa-constrictor; but two yards of thickness is scarcely credible. He writes it *dos varas de grosor*. (Grosor is thickness.) I thought the father might have meant two yards in circumference, but he afterwards says that the Indians reported them of three and four yards in diameter (*de diametro*).

We had a fresh squall of wind and rain from the northward and

101

eastward. The Portuguese, who is a careful and timid navigator, and whose motions we follow because he is a capital caterer and has a wife along to cook for us, pulled in for the beach, and we camped for the night.

Seventy miles below Yurimaguas is Santa Cruz. This is an Indian village of a tribe called Aguanos, containing three hundred and fifty inhabitants. The lieutenant-governor is the only white man in it. The women go naked down to their hips and the children entirely so. I was quite an object of curiosity and fear to them, and they seemed never tired of examining my spectacles.

I obtained at this place the sap of a large tree called *catao* which is said to be very poisonous. It appears to be acid and acts like a powerful caustic. The man who chopped the bark, to let the sap run, always turned away his face as he struck, for fear of its getting into his eyes. The Indians employ it for the purpose of curing old sores. The tree is generally very large and has a smooth bark with knots on it bearing short thorns. The leaf is nearly circular. It is called *assacu* in Brazil and is there thought to be a remedy for leprosy. We gathered also some leaves and root of a running plant called *guaco,* which, steeped in spirits and applied internally and externally, is said to be an antidote to the bite of a snake. I think it probable that this may be a fancy of the Indians, originating from the fact that the leaf has something the appearance and color of a snake-skin.

We found difficulty in getting canoes at this place. The only one that would accommodate ourselves and baggage belonged to the church. We bargained for it with the curaca (chief of the Indians, and second in authority to the lieutenant-governor); but when the lieutenant returned from his chacra, where he had been setting out plantains, he refused to let us have it on the ground that it wanted repairs. We were, therefore, obliged to take two small ones that would barely carry the trunks and boxes, and embark ourselves in the canoe of the Portuguese.

We have found this man, Don Antonio da Costa Viana, and his family quite a treasure to us on the road. He is a stout, active

102

little fellow, about fifty years of age, with piercing black eyes, long black curls, a face burned almost black by the sun, deeply pitted with the small-pox, and with a nose that, as Ijurra tells him, would make a cut-water for a frigate. He is called *paraguá* (a species of parrot) from his incessant talk, and he brags that he is "as well known on the river as a dog." He has a chacra of sugar-cane and tobacco at Tarapoto. He sells the spirits that he makes for tocuyo, and carries the tocuyo, tobacco, and chancaca to Nauta, selling and exchanging as he goes. His canoe is fifty feet long and three broad and carries a cargo which he values at five hundred dollars; that is, five hundred in *efectos*—two hundred and fifty in money. It is well fitted with armayari and pamacari, and carries six peons as well as Antonio himself, his wife, and his adopted daughter, a child of ten years. My friend is perfect master of all around him; knows all the reaches and beaches of the river and every tree and shrub that grows upon its banks. He is intelligent, active, obliging, and always busy—now twisting fishing-lines of the fibres of a palm called *chambira;* now hunting turtle-eggs, robbing plantain-fields, or making me cigars of tobacco-leaves given me by the priest of Chasuta. Every beach is a house for him. His peons build his rancho and spread his mosquito curtain; his wife and child cook his supper. His mess of salt fish, turtle-eggs, and plantains is a feast for him; and his gourd of coffee, and pipe afterwards, a luxury that a king might envy. He is always well and happy. I imagine he has picked up and hoarded away, to keep him in his old age, or to leave his wife when he dies, some few of the dollars that are floating about here. In short, I don't know a more enviable person. It is true Doña Antonio gets drunk occasionally, but he licks her if she is troublesome and she seems to give him very little concern.

September 1. Heavy clouds and rains both to the northward and eastward and southward and westward, with an occasional spit at us; but we set the rain at defiance under the palm-thatched roof of Antonio. At half-past 3 P.M. we arrived at Laguna. This town, the principal one of the district and the residence of the governor, is one and a half miles from the port. The walk is a pleasant one through the forest at this season, but is probably mud to the knees in the rains. It contains one thousand and forty-four inhabitants; the products of the neighborhood are wax, sarsaparilla, copal, copaiba, and salt fish. I have seen all these in the hands of the Indians, but in small quantities, there being so little demand for them.

September 2. Waiting for boats and boatmen. There are no large canoes and we are again compelled to take two. I was surprised at this as I was led to believe—and I thought it probable—that the nearer we got to the Marañon the larger we should find the boats, and the means of navigation more complete. But I have met with nothing but misstatements in my whole course. The impression I received in Lima of the Montaña was that it was a country abounding not only with the necessaries but with the luxuries of life, so far as eating was concerned. Yet I am now satisfied that if one hundred men were to start without provisions, on the route I have travelled, the half must inevitably perish for want of food. Of meat there is almost none; even salt fish, yuccas, and plantains are scarce, and often not to be had; game is shy; and the fish, of which there are a great number, do not readily take the hook; of fruit I have seen literally none edible since leaving Huanuco.

At Chasuta I was assured that I should find at Yurimaguas every facility for the prosecution of my journey; yet I could get neither a boat nor a man, and had to persuade my Chasuta boatmen to carry me on to Santa Cruz, where the Yurimaguas people said there would be no further difficulty. At Santa Cruz I could get but two small and rotten canoes, with three men to each, for Laguna, which, being the great port of the river, could in the estimation of the people at Santa Cruz, furnish me with the means of crossing the Atlantic if necessary. I had been always assured that I could get at Laguna one hundred Cocamillas, if I wanted them, as a force to enter among the savages of the Ucayali; but here, too, I could with difficulty get six men and two small canoes.

We found at the port of Laguna two travelling merchants, a Portuguese and a Brazilian. They had four large boats of about eight tons each, and two or three canoes. Their cargo consisted of iron, steel, iron implements, crockery-ware, wine, brandy, copper kettles, coarse, short swords (a very common implement of the Indians), guns, ammunition, salt fish, &c., which they expected to exchange in Moyobamba and Chachapoyas for straw-hats, tocuyo, sugar, coffee, and money. They were also buying up all the sarsaparilla they could find and despatching it back in canoes. They estimated the value of their cargoes at five thousand dollars. I have no doubt that two thousand dollars in money would have bought the whole concern, boats and all. They invited us to breakfast off roast pig, and I thought that I never tasted anything better than the *farinha* which I saw and tasted for the first time.

Farinha is a general substitute for bread in all the region of the Amazon below the Brazilian frontier. It is used by all classes and in immense quantities by the Indians and laborers. Our boat-men in Brazil were always contented with plenty of salt fish and farinha. Every two or three hours of the day, while travelling, they would stop rowing, pour a little water upon a large gourd-full of farinha, and pass around the mass (which they called *pirào*) as if it were a delicacy.

The women generally make the farinha. They soak the root of the mandioc (Jatropha Manihot) in water till it is softened a little, when they scrape off the skin, and grate it upon a board smeared with some of the adhesive gums of the forest and sprinkled with pebbles. The white grated mass is put in a conical-shaped bag, made of the coarse fibres of a palm and called *tapiti*. The bag is hung up to a peg driven into a tree or a post of the shed; a lever is put through a loop at the bottom of the bag; the short end of the lever is placed under a chock nailed to the post below, and the woman hangs her weight on the long end. This elongates the bag, and brings a heavy pressure upon the mass within, causing all the juice to ooze out through the interstices of the wicker-work of the bag. When sufficiently pressed, the mass is put on the floor of a mud oven. Heat is applied, and it is stirred with a stick till it granulates in very irregular grains (the largest about the size of our No. 2 shot) and is sufficiently toasted to drive off all the poisonous qualities which it has in a crude state. It is then packed in baskets (lined and covered with palm-leaves) of about sixty-four pounds weight, which are generally sold, all along the river, at from seventy-five cents to one dollar. The sediment of the juice which runs from the tapiti is tapioca, and is used to make custards, puddings, starch, &c.

September 3. Our boatmen came down to the port at 8 A.M. They were accompanied, as usual, by their wives, carrying their bedding, their jars of masato, and even their paddles. These fellows are too lazy to do a hand's turn when on shore, though when embarked they work freely, and are gay, cheerful, ready, and obedient. The dress of the women is nothing more than a piece of cotton cloth, generally dark brown in color, wrapped around the loins and reaching to the knee. I was struck with the appearance of one, the only pretty Indian girl I have seen. She appeared to be about thirteen years of age, and was the wife of one of our boatmen. It was amusing to see the slavish respect with which she waited upon the young savage (himself about nineteen), and the lordly indifference with which he received her attentions. She was as straight as an arrow, delicately and elegantly formed, and had a free, wild, Indian look that was quite taking.

We got off at a quarter past nine; the merchants at the same time. The padre also returns to-day to Yurimaguas, so that we made quite a haul upon the population of Laguna, and carried off about seventy of its inhabitants. Twenty-five miles below Laguna, we arrived at the mouth of the Huallaga. Several islands occupy the middle of it. The Huallaga, just above the islands, is three hundred and fifty yards wide; the Amazon, at the junction, five hundred. The water of both rivers is very muddy and filthy.

CHAPTER VIII

Entrance into the Amazon—Nauta—Don Bernardino—River Ucayali

* * *

The river upon which we now entered is the main trunk of the Amazon, which carries its Peruvian name of Marañon as far as the Brazilian frontier; below which, and as far as the junction of the Rio Negro, it takes the name of Solimões; and thence to the ocean is called Amazon. It is the same stream throughout, and, to avoid confusion, I shall call it Amazon from this point to the sea.

The march of the great river in its silent grandeur was sublime, but in the untamed might of its turbid waters, as they cut away its banks and tore down the gigantic denizens of the forest, it was awful. I was reminded of our Mississippi at its topmost flood. The waters are quite as muddy and quite as turbid, but this stream lacked the charm and the fascination which the plantation upon the bank, the city upon the bluff, and the steamboat upon its waters lends to its fellow of the North; nevertheless, I felt pleased at its sight. I had already travelled seven hundred miles by water, and fancied that this powerful stream would soon carry me to the ocean; but the water-travel was comparatively just begun; many a weary month was to elapse ere I should again look upon the familiar face of the sea; and many a time, when worn and wearied with canoe life, did I exclaim, "This river seems interminable!"

September 4. The shores of the river are low, but abrupt. The lower strata next to the water's edge are of sand, hardening into rock. There were a great many porpoises sporting in the river. At 3 P.M. we passed the narrow arm of the river that runs by Urarinas, a small village situated on the left bank. The channel inside the island seemed nearly dry. Ijurra, however, passed through it in a small canoe, and bought some fowls and a small monkey at the pueblo. The channel of the river runs near the right bank. Population of Urarinas, eighty.

September 5. The *patos reales,* a large and beautiful species of duck with which the river abounds, are now breeding. We saw numbers of pairs conducting their broods over the water. Though the young ones could not fly, they could dive so long and fast that we could not catch them. I find that they answer exactly to the description of the Egyptian goose. They have small horns on their wings.

September 6. Passed the mouth of the small river Airico on the left. One of our Indians says that the ascent of this river for a week brings the traveller to a lake, and for another week, to a range of mountains.

We have had quite heavy squalls of wind and rain every day since entering the Amazon. The canoes are so low that they cannot ride the waves of mid-river, and we are compelled to pull for the land and wait for the storm to pass. We saw alligators to-day for the first time.

September 7. Arrived at Parinari. This is an Indian village of three hundred and thirty inhabitants, situated on a hill on the right bank of the river. It is about twenty feet above the present level of the river, which rises, in the full, to within three feet of the houses. The people live principally by fishing and gathering sarsaparilla. The lieutenant-governor gave us some spirits made of plantains. It was vile stuff, very strong.

September 8. The Fiscales killed six howling monkeys with their blow-guns. Passed the mouth of Tigre Yacu on the left. It is seventy yards broad, and looks deep and free from obstruction. Its waters are much clearer than those of the Amazon. It is navigable for canoes a long way up, and a considerable quantity

108

of sarsaparilla is gathered on its banks which are inhabited by savages who are said to be warlike and dangerous. We camped at night on an island near the middle of the river. A narrow island lay between us and a small pueblo on the left bank, whence we could hear the sound of music and merry-making throughout the night.

September 9. Passed a channel called Pucati, which is a small mouth of the Ucayali. It is now nearly dry. In the rainy season it is passable for canoes, but it spreads out so much in its course (forming small lakes) that it leaves few places to kindle a fire on, or sleep. For this reason it is little used. Soon after leaving this, we passed another small channel, said to communicate with a large lake. We arrived at Nauta at noon, having travelled two hundred and ten miles from the mouth of the Huallaga.

We called on the governor general of the Missions of Mainas, Don José Maria Arebalo, who received us with some formality, and gave us lodgings in one of the houses of the village, turning out the inhabitants, I suspect, for that purpose. My companion, Ijurra, was not sure of a cordial reception, for, when sub-prefect of the province, he had caused Arebalo to be arrested. But our friend was much too magnanimous to remember old feuds, and he and Ijurra soon became boon companions.

Nauta is a fishing village of one thousand inhabitants, mostly Indians of the Cocama tribe. It has a few white residents engaged in trading with the Indians for salt fish, wax, and sarsaparilla. Don Bernardino Cauper, an old Portuguese, does most of the business of the place. He sends parties of Indians to fish or gather sarsaparilla upon the Napo and Ucayali, and he has two or three boats (called in this part of the country *garreteas*) trading down the river.

Don Bernardino lives in a sort of comfort. He has plenty of meat (calling turtle, salt fish, and fowls meat), with farinha from below and beans and onions from his little garden. There is good tobacco from above to smoke, and wholesome, though fiery, Lisbon wine to drink. I have been frequently struck during my journey with the comparative value of things. The humblest man of a village of one thousand inhabitants in the United States would think Bernardino's table poorly supplied and would turn up his nose at a grass hammock slung between two hooks in the shop for a bed-place. Yet these things were regal luxuries to us, and, doubtless, being the best that are to be had, Don Bernardino is perfectly contented and desires nothing better.

The old gentleman is very pious. The Cura of Pebas was at this time in Nauta, attending to the repairs of the church, and we celebrated a nine-days' service in honor of our Lady of Mercy, the patroness of the arms of Peru. The expenses of the service (being a fee for the padre and the lighting of the church with wax) were borne by individuals. The padre gave the first day; then Senhor Cauper; then his wife, his wife's sister, his son, and his pretty Brazilian niece, Dona Candida; then came Arebalo; then Ijurra and I; the priest winding up on Sunday. But my old friend was not contented with this. When I shoved off on Monday for the Ucayali, I left him engaged in another church service, setting off rockets and firing, from time to time, an old blunderbuss loaded to the muzzle, in honor of a miracle that had happened in Rimini, in Italy, about a year and a half ago, of which he had just received intelligence.

Don Bernardino has four or five slaves in his house—blacks, which he brought from Brazil. This is contrary to the law, but it is winked at; I heard the governor say that he would like much to have a pair. Don Bernardino said they would be difficult to get and would cost him five hundred dollars in money. A slave that is a mechanic is worth five hundred dollars in Brazil.

Arebalo, the governor general, gave us specimens of the woods of the country; they are called *aguano, ishpingo, muena, capirono, cedro, palo de cruz* (our lignum-vitae, and *palo de sangre* —all good, whether for house- or ship-building; and some of them very hard, heavy, and beautiful. The palo de sangre is of a rich red color, susceptible of a high polish, and a decoction of its bark is said to be good to stay bloody evacuations. I had no opportunity

110

of testing it, but suspect it is given on the homoeopathic principle that "like cures like" because it is red.

The temperature of Nauta is agreeable. The lowest thermometer I observed was 71° at 6 A.M., and the highest 89° at 3 P.M. We have had a great deal of cloudy weather and rain since we have been on the Amazon, and it is now near the beginning of the rainy season at this place. No one suffers from heat, though this is probably the hottest season of the year and heavy squalls of wind and rain sweep over the country almost every day. The town is situated on a hill, with the forest well cleared away from around it, and is a healthy place. I saw only two cases of sickness during my stay of two weeks. They were acute cases of disease, to which people are liable everywhere. Both died, probably for want of medical attention.

The Cocamas of Nauta are great fishermen and boatmen. I think they are bolder than most of the civilized tribes on the river. They make incursions, now and then, into the country of the Mayorunas—savages who inhabit the right banks of the Ucayali and Amazon—fight battles with them, and bring home prisoners. When travelling in small numbers, or engaged in their ordinary avocations on the river, they studiously avoid the country of their enemies, who retaliate whenever opportunity offers. These Indians are jealous and punish conjugal infidelity with severity, as well as departure from the laws of chastity on the part of the unmarried female.

A boat came in from above on the eighteenth and reported the loss of another belonging to one of the traders we had met at Laguna. She was loaded with salt and cotton cloth, and, in passing the mouth of Tigre Yacu in the night, struck upon a "sawyer," capsized, and went down. A boy was drowned. Macready would have envied the low, soft, sad tones and eloquent gestures, expressive of pity and horror, with which an Indian told us the disastrous story.

September 20. We paid twelve rowers and a popero and set them to work to fit up our boat with decks and coverings. I had

111

purchased this boat from Don Bernardino for sixty dollars, the price he paid for it when it was new. Most persons on the river held up their hands when I told them what I had paid for it, but I thought it was cheap, especially as I was obliged to have it on any terms. He had it repaired and calked for us.

The boat is thirty feet long, seven wide in its widest part, and three deep. The after-part is decked for about ten feet in length with the bark of a palm-tree, which is stripped from the trunk and flattened out by force. The deck is covered over by small poles, bent in hoop-fashion over it, and well thatched with palm-leaves, making quite a snug little cabin. The pilot stands or sits on this roof to direct and steer, and sleeps upon it at night, to the manifest danger of rolling off. About twelve feet of the middle of the boat is covered and decked in like manner, but the covering is lower and narrower, giving room for the rowers to sit on each side of it to paddle. Most of the cargo is stowed under the decks, thus leaving a cabin for both Ijurra and myself. There is a space between the two coverings which is not decked over that gives a chance for bailing the boat when she takes in water, and a sufficient space is left in the bow on which to place a large earthen vessel to make a fire in.

I also bought from Don Bernardino some Portuguese axes, some small fish-hooks (called by the Indians *mishqui*), and some white beads, which are most coveted by the savages of the Ucayali.

September 25. Having engaged a servant named Lopez and embarked our luggage and provisions, I hoisted a small American flag and got under way for the Ucayali. We started with ten peons, but were joined by two others in a skiff next morning. In fifty-five minutes we arrived at the mouth of the Ucayali. It is a beautiful stream, with low, shelving, green banks at its mouth. But I was disappointed in its size; it was not more than half as wide as the Amazon. It is the longest known tributary above Brazil, and is therefore called by some the main trunk of the Amazon. We poled and paddled slowly up the left bank for four and a half miles, and stopped at a bluff where there were one or two huts of people. Rain threatening, we attempted to sleep in the boat, but our mosquito curtains not being properly prepared we passed a wretched night.

September 26. Taking advantage of the eddies and still water near the shore, we paddled and poled along at about the rate of a mile and a half per hour. Our men work well. They commence paddling with a strong, slow stroke, of about fifteen or twenty to the minute, and gradually quicken them till they get to be half-second strokes. They keep this up for about half an hour, when, at a shout from the bowman, they toss their paddles in the air, change sides, and commence the slow stroke again. They, however, prefer poling to paddling, and will always make for a beach, where they can use their poles, which they do in a lazy, inefficient manner.

After breakfast we pulled nearly to the middle of the river, and, anchoring in thirty-three feet water, we found the current, by the log, to be a mile and three-quarters the hour. We passed the mouth of a small stream called Chingana, up which there is a settlement of the Mayorunas. Our men are much afraid of this people and always sleep on the left bank so long as they are in their country. All the peons on this river have their mosquito curtains painted black so that the Mayorunas may not see them in the night. The mode of attack of these savages is to wait till the travellers have fallen asleep and then rush upon the mosquito nets and plunge in their lances. None of the Indians that I have travelled with seem to have any idea of the propriety of posting a sentinel.

September 27. Two of our turtles died yesterday, and the Indians are eating them to-day. Ijurra suspects that they killed them, but Ijurra is of a suspicious nature, especially where Indians are concerned. We found the current to-day to be two miles the hour. A fish about two feet long, and sharp-built, like a dolphin, jumped into the boat. It had two curved and very sharp teeth, like those of a squirrel, or the fangs of a serpent, in the lower jaw. It made us a very good mess.

113

September 28. Passed the outlet of a lake said to be a day distant. There are many lakes on each side of the river where the Indians fish with barbasco. At this season most of the outlets are dry. Passed two balsas loaded with sarsaparilla. One was in charge of a Brazilian Negro, the other of a Portuguese. The crew were Conibos Indians of the Ucayali. They had a floating turtle-pen along and gave us a turtle. When we stopped to breakfast, our people hid their jars, which they had emptied of their masata, to pick up on the return. Banks of the river, as usual, about ten or fifteen feet high. Beaches few and small, running out in ridges, so that at one moment our men could not touch bottom with their long poles, and at the next the boat was aground.

September 29. We passed a place in the river where there was a beach on each side and a tree grounded in the middle. On the side which we passed, which was to the right of the tree, we had but four feet water sixty yards from the beach. I suspect the tree was grounded on a sand-flat at the upper end of an island. Passed the mouth of the Canõ Pucati, which communicates with the Marañon just below San Regis. It is now entirely dry, and appears a mere fissure in the bank between the cane and small trees growing near it. The sand which is heaped up at its entrance is four feet above the present level of the river.

Stopped and bought some turtle, salt, and salted *curassows* (a large, black, game bird, nearly the size, and with something the appearance, of our native turkey) from some San Regis people, who were salting fish which they had taken in a lake nearby. Their ranchos were built on a bluff on the right bank. I could not stay among them for the mosquitoes and had to retreat to the boat. Two large turtles, three salted birds, and half a peck of salt cost us six strings of small beads.

September 30. Passed the mouth of an arm of the river which is said to leave the main river many miles above and make the large island of Paynaco. It is navigable for canoes in the wet season but on account of its windings it takes nearly as long to pass it as it does to pass the main river. We saw many cranes and

114

huananas (the Egyptian goose before described), but no animals except flesh-colored porpoises, of which there are a great many. Occasionally we hear *cotomonos,* or howling monkeys, in the woods. Dull work ascending the river. Anchored near low sand islands with abrupt banks, which were continually tumbling into the stream.

October 1. After daylight we landed and shot at cotomonos. One is not aware of the great height of the trees until he attempts to shoot a monkey or a bird out of the topmost branches. He is then surprised to find that the object is entirely out of reach of his fowling-piece and that only a rifle will reach it. The trees throughout this country grow with great rapidity, and, being in a light, thin soil, with a substratum of sand, the roots are superficial and the trees are continually falling down. Nature seems to have made a provision for their support, for, instead of coming down round to the ground, the trunk, about ten feet above it, divides into thick, wide tablets, which widening as they come down, stand out like buttresses for the support of the tree; but even with this provision no day passes that we do not hear the crashing fall of some giant of the forest. Restowed the boat and repaired Ijurra's palace, making it narrower and higher.

October 3. Many huananas, with their broods, upon the river. Shot a large brown bird called *chansu* (*cigana* in Brazil). It has a crest and looks like a pheasant. Large flocks frequent the cane on the banks of the river. They have a very game look and are attractive to the sportsman, but the Indians call them a foul bird and do not eat them. The crop of this was filled with green herbage.

October 4. Clear all night, with heavy dew. The anchor, which is a sixty-four-pound weight, had sunk so deep in the thick dark sand of the bottom as to require the united exertions of all hands to get it. Met three canoes going down loaded with sarsaparilla; bought some yuccas and plantains at a settlement of five families of Conibos, on the left bank of the river. Got also specimens of the black wax of the country, and *lacre,* or sealing-wax, which is the gum of a tree, colored red with achote. The black wax is the production of a small bee very little larger than an ant, which builds its house in the ground. The white wax is deposited in the branches of a small tree, which are hollow, and divided into compartments like the joints of a cane. The wood is sufficiently soft to be perforated by the bee; the tree is called *cetica,* and looks, though larger, like our alder bush.

October 5. Stopped at a Conibo rancho on the right bank. Three men and six women, with children, were living in the rancho. They were very poor and could sell us nothing.

October 6. Passed a settlement of Conibos on left bank—four houses, eight men and twenty-five women and children. It was quite a treat to see so familiar a flower as the convolvulus growing on the bank. It was not so large or so gay as in our gardens, but had a home look that was very pleasing. Passed a ravine, up which there is a settlement of Amajuacas Indians. These men are hunters, who live in the interior, and seldom come down upon the rivers. The Pirros and Conibos sometimes make war upon them and bring away captives. Yesterday two men—one a Pano, from Sarayacu, and the other an Amajuaca—joined us to work their passage to Sarayacu. The Amajuaca was so good a fellow and worked so well that I paid him the same wage as the others.

October 7. River half a mile wide and rising fast. Trunks of trees begin to come down. Stopped at a settlement called Guanache. I saw only two houses, with four or five men and women. They said that the others were away gathering sarsaparilla. These people cannot count and I can never get from them any accurate idea of numbers. The houses were very large, measuring between thirty and forty feet in length and ten or fifteen in breadth. They consist of immense roofs of small poles and cane, thatched with palm, and supported by short stakes four feet high and three inches in diameter. Many persons live together in one of these houses. Cotton was growing here.

October 9. Stopped at the village of Santa Maria, a Pirros settlement, on the left bank, of one hundred and fifty souls.

116

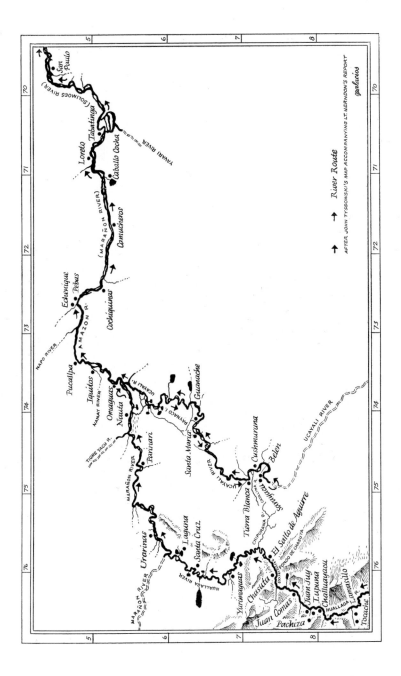

River Route

AFTER JOHN TYSSOWSKI'S MAP ACCOMPANYING LT. HERNDON'S REPORT

galerios

San Paulo

(SOLIMOES RIVER)

Tabatinga

Loreto

YAVARI RIVER

Caballo Cocha

(MARAÑON RIVER)

Camucheros

Echenique

Pebas

Cochiquinas

NAPO RIVER

AMAZON R.

Pucallpa

Iquitos

MANAY RIVER

Omaguas

Nauta

UCAYALI RIVER

PAYACO R.

Guanache

TIGRE YACU R.

Parinari

Santa Maria

MARAÑON RIVER

UCAYALI RIVER

UCAYALI RIVER

Cushmurana

Belen

Tierra Blanca

Tarapaca

Urarinas

Laguna

Santa Cruz

CHIPURANA R.

HUALLAGA RIVER

El Salto de Aguirre

Sarayaquas

Chasuta

COLLOS PONGO DE CHASUTA

Juan Comas

Juan Juy

Laguna

Chaihuayacu

Pachiza

Huallaga

Lamasillo

Tocache

There were two Moyobambinos domiciled in the village, purchasing salt fish from the Indians. One of them told me that an Indian would furnish eighty pieces of salt fish for eight yards of tocuyo; this man may have "let the cat out of the bag" and showed me how they cheat the Indians. A yard of tocuyo is the general price of three pieces. A fish called payshi, which is the fish ordinarily salted, was brought in and cut up while we were here. It is a powerful fish, about six feet long and one and one-fourth in diameter. The head is fourteen inches long, with short jaws and rather small mouth. The tongue, when dried, is as hard as bone, and is commonly used as a rasp. The scales of the belly and tail are bordered with a bright red streak, which makes the fish appear to be nearly encircled with a number of scarlet rings and gives it a very pretty appearance.

Two hours after leaving Santa Maria we arrived at a beach where there was an establishment of Don Bernardino's for salting fish. These establishments are called *factorias*. A nephew of the old man has been here for two months, attending to the business. Instead of employing the Infidels, he brings Indians of Nauta with him—people generally who are in Don Bernardino's debt. Twenty-five Indians collect and salt four thousand pieces of fish in six weeks.

The Indians on this river have in their houses cotton, maize, ground peas (*mani*), sweet potatoes, yuccas, plantains, fowls and fish, bows and arrows, lances, clubs, paddles, and pretty baskets made of cane. The women weave their own clothes and those of their husbands, and manage to paint figures and devices on the cotton after it is woven. The Conibos seem taller than they really are, on account of their costume, which is a long cotton gown. I have seen a fellow in one of these gowns, slowly striding over a beach, looking, at a distance, like a Roman patrician in his toga.

October 10. Met a Conibo, with his wife and two children, on the beach. This man was evidently the dandy of his tribe. He was painted with a broad stripe of red under each eye, and three narrow stripes of blue were carried from one ear, across the upper lip, to the other—the two lower stripes plain, the upper one bordered with figures. The whole of the lower jaw and chin were painted with a blue chain-work of figures that resembled Chinese figures. Around his neck was a broad tight necklace of black and white beads, with a breastplate of the same hanging from it and partly concealed by his long gown. His wrists were also adorned with wide bracelets of white beads, above which were bracelets of lizard skins, set round with monkeys' teeth. He wore a little silver shield hanging from his nose, and a narrow, thin plate of silver, shaped like a paddle, two and a half inches long, thrust through a hole in the lower lip, hanging on his chin. He had been to Cuzco, where he got his silver ornaments, and said it was a journey of four moons. We anchored in thirty-six feet water, and found a current of three miles the hour. Calm, clear night; much dew.

October 11. Stopped to breakfast on a beach on the left bank, back of which, on the firm land, were two houses of Remos Indians. There were twenty-two of them—men, women, and children—with three men of the Shipebos tribe. There seemed to be no uniformity in their paint, each one consulting his own taste; though there was one man and a woman, whom I understood to be man and wife, painted exactly alike. The Remos were low and small; the Shipebos taller. They dress in the common costume of the Ucayali and have their hair cut straight across the forehead, just above the eyes, so as to show the face, set, as it were, in a frame of hair. Passed more huts afterwards and some Indians seeking the young of the turtle on a beach. These people eat anything. I have known them to eat the eggs of the turtle with the young in them, and also turtle that had died a natural death and had become offensive.

October 13. At breakfast we found a smaller kind of turtle called *charapilla,* better and more tender than the large turtle which is called *charapa.* Stopped at a little settlement of Shipebos on the right bank—twenty-five all told. Met three Negroes, with a crew of Conibos, who had been up the river for sarsaparilla. Passed two houses of Conibos, about fifteen in number. One of them, taking us for padres, insisted that Ijurra should baptize his child, which was accordingly done. He gave it the name of the officiating priest, writing it on a bit of paper and giving it to the mother, who put it away carefully. I believe my companion was later upbraided by a real priest for doing so. The head of the infant had been bound in boards, front and rear, and was flattened and increased in height. I do not observe that the heads of the adults bear any trace of this custom.

October 15. Arrived at the village of Tierra Blanca, having passed yesterday several settlements of Indians. It is a clean little town of two hundred inhabitants, situated on an eminence on the left bank about twenty-five feet above the present level of the river. In full stage the water approaches within a few feet of the lower houses.

A priest from Sarayacu, Father Juan de Dios Lorente, has charge of the spiritual and pretty much of the temporal concerns of the village. He is here at this time celebrating some feast and is the only white man present. The Indians, as usual at a feast time, were nearly all drunk and made my men drunk also. When I wished to start, I sent Ijurra to a large house where they were drinking to bring our people to the boat; he soon came back, foaming with rage, and demanded a gun, that he might bring them to obedience. I soothed him, however, and went up to the house, where, by taking a drink with them, and practising the arts that I have often practised before in getting back to the ship refractory sailors who were drinking on shore, I succeeded in persuading a sufficient number of them to work the boat, and shoved off with as drunk a crew as one could desire, leaving the small boat for the others to follow; this they are sure to do when they find that their clothes and bedding have been taken away. The padre said that if Ijurra had shot one, they would have murdered us all. I doubt that. We were well armed and the Indians are afraid of guns.

October 16. Started at 6 A.M.; stopped at half-past five opposite the mouth of the river Catalina. It seemed thirty yards wide and had a small island in front. The ascent of the river is very tedious. We barely creep along against a force of the current and day after day goes by in the most monotonous routine. I frequently land, and with gun on shoulder, clad only in shirt and drawers, walk for miles along the beaches. My greatest pleasure is to watch the boat struggling up against the tide. This is always accompanied with emotions of pride, mingled with a curious and scarcely definable feeling of surprise. It was almost startling to see, at her mast-head, the well-beloved flag of my country dancing in the breeze on the waters of the strange river and waving above the heads of the swarthy and grim figures below. I felt a proud affection for it; I had carried it where it had never been before; there was a bond between us; we were alone in a strange land; it and I were brothers in the wilderness.

October 17. Met ten canoes of Conibos—twenty-eight men, women and children who had been on an excursion, with no particular object, as far as the first stones in the Ucayali. This is about thirty-eight days above Sarayacu, at a place called Rumi Callarina, or commencement of the rocks. River rising for the last two or three days. Passed a village of Shipebos, called Cushmuruna; hills in sight, bearing south.

October 18. At 11 A.M. we entered the caño of Sarayacu; at this season this is not more than fifteen or eighteen feet wide, and nearly covered with a tall grass something like broom-corn or a small species of cane. The caño has as much as six feet depth in the middle for two miles, but it soon contracts so as scarcely to allow room for my boat to pass and becomes shallow and obstructed with the branches of small trees which bend over it. Also, about two miles from its mouth, it changes its character of caño, or arm of the main river, and becomes the little river of Sarayacu, which retires and advances in accordance with the movements of its great neighbor.

We could not get our boat nearer than within a quarter of a mile of Sarayacu, so we took small canoes from the bank and carried up our gear in them. We were hospitably received by the padres and lodgings were given us in their dwelling, a large house with several rooms in it.

We found Sarayacu a rather neat-looking Indian village, of about one thousand inhabitants; this includes those who live in Belen, a small town of one hundred and fifty inhabitants, one and a half mile distant. The missionary station—including, besides Sarayacu, the towns of Santa Catalina and Tierra Blanca—is governed by four Franciscan friars. The principal and prefect, Padre Juan Chrisostomo Cimini, being now absent, the general direction is left in the hands of Father Vicente Calvo, assisted by the Fathers Bregati and Lorente, who have charge, respectively, of Santa Catalina and Tierra Blanca.

Father Calvo, meek and humble in personal concerns, yet full of zeal and spirit for his office, clad in his long serge gown, belted with a cord, with bare feet and accurate tonsure, habitual stoop, and generally bearing upon his shoulder a beautiful and saucy bird of the parrot kind, called *chiriclis,* was my beau ideal of a missionary monk. He is an Arragonese and had served as a priest in the army of Don Carlos. Bregati is a young and handsome Italian, whom Father Calvo sometimes calls St. John. Lorente was a tall, grave, and cold-looking Catalan. A lay-brother named Maquin, who did the cooking and who was unwearied in his attentions to us, made up the establishment. I was sick here and think that I shall ever remember with gratitude the affectionate kindness of these pious and devoted friars of St. Francis.

The padres have recently obtained an order giving them the exclusive right of collecting sarsaparilla on the Ucayali and its tributaries, but I doubt if this will benefit them much; there being no power to enforce the decree, the Portuguese will send their agents there as before.

Each padre has two Mitayo Indians—one a hunter, the other a fisherman—to supply his table with the products of the forest and the river. The government is paternal. The Indians recognize in the padre the power to appoint and remove officers; to inflict stripes; and to confine in the stocks. They obey the priest's orders readily and seem tractable and docile. They take advantage, however, of Father Calvo's good nature, and are sometimes a little insolent. On an occasion of this kind, my friend Ijurra, who is always an advocate of strong measures and says that in the government of the Indians there is nothing like the *santo palo* (sacred cudgel), asked Father Calvo why he did not put the impudent rascal in the stocks. But the good Father replied that he did not like to do it—that it was cruel and hurt the poor fellow's legs.

The Indians here, as elsewhere, are drunken and lazy. The women do most of the work; carry most of the burdens to and from the fields and canoes; make the masato and the earthen vessels out of which it is drunk; spin the cotton and weave the cloth; cook and take care of the children. And their reward is to be maltreated by their husbands, and, in their drunken frolics, to be cruelly beaten and sometimes badly wounded.

The town is very healthy, there being no endemics, but only acute attacks from great exposure or imprudence in eating and drinking. From the parish register it appears that in the year 1850 there were ten marriages, sixty-two births, and twenty-four deaths. From an examination of the other years, this appears to be a pretty fair average; yet the population is constantly decreasing. Father Calvo attributes this to desertion. He says that many go down the Amazon with passengers and cargoes, and, finding the return difficult, they settle either in the villages upon the river or join the Ticumas and other Infidel tribes and never come back.

Spaniards from the Huallaga also frequently buy the young Indians from their parents and carry them off for domestic services at home. Father Calvo spoke with great indignation of this custom and said if he could catch any person stealing his people he would hang him in the plaza. Thus Sarayacu is becoming depopulated in spite of the paternal kindness and mild government of Father Calvo. My own impression as to the reason of their desertion is not that it is on account of the difficulties of the return, or indifference, or a proclivity to fall back into savage life; but that the missionaries have civilized the Indians in some degree—have awakened in their minds ambition and a desire to improve their condition. For this reason the Indian leaves Sarayacu and goes to Brazil. In Sarayacu there are comparatively none to employ him and pay for his services. In Brazil, the Portuguese *commerciante*, though he maltreats him and does not give him enough to eat, pays him for his labor. Thus he accumulates, becomes a man of property, and in the course of time possibly returns to his family in possession of a wooden trunk painted blue, with a lock and key to it, and filled with hatchets, knives, beads, fish-hooks, mirrors, &c. He has seen the world and is an object of envy to his kinsmen and neighbors.

The friars entertained us on Sunday evening with a dance of Indians. These were dressed in frocks and trousers, and had headdresses made of a bandeau or circlet of short and rich-colored feathers surmounted with the long tail-feathers of the scarlet macaw. Around their legs they had strings of dried nut shells, which made an agreeable jingling in the dance. The half-bent knee and graceful wave of the plumed hat towards the priest before the dance commenced, with the regularity of the figure, gave unmistakable evidence of the teaching of the padres who appear to have neglected nothing, however trivial, that might bind the affections of the proselytes.

The inhabitants of Sarayacu are divided into three distinct tribes, called Panos, Omaguas, and Yameos. They dwell in different parts of the town. Each tribe has its peculiar dialect, but they generally communicate in the Pano language. The Yameos are the whitest and best-looking Indians I have seen. I was unable to gather much authentic information concerning the Infidels of the Ucayali. The padres had only been in Sarayacu a few years and had never left their post to travel among the Indians. The Campas are the most numerous and warlike tribe and are resolute in forbidding strangers to enter their territory. They inhabit all the upper waters of the Ucayali and I think it probable that they are the same who, under the name of Chunchos, are so hostile to the whites about Chanchamayo and on the haciendas to the eastward of Cuzco. These are the people who, under Juan Santos Atahaulpa, in 1742, swept away all the Missions of the Cerro de la Sal, and I have very little doubt that they are descendants of the Inca race. From the extent of their territory, one might judge them to be the most numerous body of savages in America. No estimate can be formed of their numbers, however, as no one capable of making one ever ventures among them.

When I left Nauta, I intended to ascend the Ucayali, as far as Chanchamayo if possible, and also to examine the Pachitea. On arriving at Sarayacu, I consulted Father Calvo on the subject. He at first spoke discouragingly, saying that the larger part of the population of his village were away fishing and that I would have great difficulty in recruiting a sufficient number of men for the expedition. He told me that Padre Cimini, year before last, with a complement of one hundred and fifty men, had been beaten back by the Campas when within one day of Jesus Maria, at the confluence of the Pangoa and Perene, and had declared it was folly to attempt the trip with a less number of men, and these well armed. Father Calvo also said that, could he raise the men by contributions from Tierra Blanca and Santa Catalina, he could not possibly furnish provisions for half that number. I told him I was ready to start with twenty-five men—fifteen for my own boat, ten for a lighter canoe to act as an advanced guard—and to depend upon the river itself for support; that I had no idea of invading the Infidel country or forcing a passage; and that the moment I met with resistance, or want of provisions, I would return.

Upon this reasoning the padre said he would do his best and sent off expresses to Fathers Bregati and Lorente with instructions to recruit men in Tierra Blanca and Santa Catalina and send them, with what provisions could be mustered, to Sarayacu. In the meantime we commenced beating up recruits and gave orders

126

to make farinha, gather barbasco for fishing on the route, and distil aguadiente.

We found, however, although I offered double pay, that we could not get more than eight men in Sarayacu who were willing to go at this season. Many of the Sarayacu people had been with Father Cimini on his expedition. They said that the current was then so strong that when the river was low they were forced to drag the canoes by ropes along the beaches; that now the current was stronger and the river so full that there were no beaches, and consequently no places for sleeping or on which to make fires for cooking. In short, they made a thousand excuses for not going, but I think the principal reason was fear of the Campas.

Fathers Bregati and Lorente reported that they could not raise a man, so that I saw myself obliged to abandon the expedition upon which I had rather set my heart. I felt, in turning my boat's head down stream, that the pleasure and excitement of the expedition were passed; that I was done, and had done nothing. I became ill and dispirited and never fairly recovered the gaiety of temper and elasticity of spirit which had animated me at the start until I received the congratulations of my friends at home.

CHAPTER IX

Upper Ucayali—Departure from Sarayacu—Omaguas—Adventures of Ijurra—Iquitos—Mouth of the Napo—Pebas—San José de los Yaguas

*　*　*

I could get any number of men for the voyage down, and on October 28th, at 10 A.M., we left Sarayacu and dropped down to the mouth of the caño, where we stopped to re-stow and shake things together. We found the Ucayali a very different-looking stream from what it was when we left it; much higher, with a stronger current, and covered with many floating trees. At 3 P.M. we took leave of good Father Calvo with much regret and started in company with Father Bregati (who was returning to Catalina), and with a large canoe that we were carrying down for the return of our peons from Pebas. I was much pleased with our new men, particularly with our pilot, old Andres Urquia, a long, hard-weather, Tom-Coffin-looking fellow, whom travel and exposure for many years seemed to have hardened into a being insensible to fatigue and impervious to disease. He has navigated the rivers of the country a great deal and was with Father Cimini when driven back by the Campas.

We passed the distance from Sarayacu to Nauta in eight days, which had cost us twenty-three in the ascent. The distance from Sarayacu to the mouth is two hundred and seventy miles. We travelled all one night when near the mouth, but this is dangerous on the Ucayali and Huallaga. The channels on these rivers are frequently obstructed by grounded trees, striking one of which

128

the boat would almost inevitably perish. It is safer on the broader Amazon.

I had intended to stay at Nauta some days, for I found that so much canoe life was beginning to affect my health and that I was getting weaker day by day, but Nauta seemed a different place than when I left it. Arebalo, the priest, and Antonio, the paragua, were gone, and Don Bernardino seemed out of humor and not glad to see us. I expect the old gentleman was troubled in his mind about his fish. He had three thousand pieces on a beach of the Ucayali, with the river rising fast and threatening its safety; his boats had just got off to fetch them away and were travelling very slowly upstream.

I wished to get a few more peons, but there were no authorities and the Indians were engaged in drinking and dancing. Two of my men, whom I had picked up at a settlement called Santos Guagua, on the Ucayali, deserted, though paid as far as Pebas. I feared to lose more, and so, collecting the few birds and animals I had left here, I started at half-past 5 P.M. on the 5th of November, having slept in my boat on the night of the 4th for the want of a house and being nearly devoured by the mosquitoes.

I left Lopez, the servant, who had only engaged for the Ucayali trip, and two of my Sarayacu people, who were reported to have gone into the woods to gather chambira, but who I suspected were drinking with the Cocamas and did not wish to be found. We drifted with the current all night. The soundings at the mouth of the Ucayali were forty-two feet. The Amazon looked grand in the moonlight below the island of Omaguas, where I judged it to be a mile and a half wide.

November 6. We arrived at Omaguas at 5 A.M. It is situated on a height on the left bank and is screened from the river, at this season, by a small island which is covered in the full. The entrance now is by a narrow creek to the southward of the town. The number of inhabitants is two hundred and thirty-two, of the tribes of Omaguas and Panos. They are peons and fishermen; cultivate chacras; and live in the usual filthy and wretched condition of all these people. I gave some calomel, salts, and spermaceti ointment to the governor's wife, who was a pitiable object —a mere skeleton and covered with sores. I was reminded of Lazarus, or old Job in his misery. I doubt if my remedies were of the proper sort, but she and her husband were anxious to have them.

Left Omaguas at a quarter past nine. At noon, moderate breeze from the northward and eastward. Thermometer 86°. As I write this, most of the men and animals are fast asleep. Even the monkeys, except one who is known hereabouts as a "friar" and who seems as sleepless as I, are dozing. The friar gapes and closes his eyes now and then, but at the next instant appears to have discovered something strange or new and is as wide awake and alert as if he never slept.

There was a great disturbance among the animals this morning. The *Pumagarza,* or tiger crane (from being speckled and colored like the tiger of the country), with a bill as long and sharp as an Infidel's spear, has picked to pieces the head of a delicate sort of turkey-hen, called *Pava del Monte.* The *Diputado* (as we call a white monkey, because Ijurra says he is the exact image of the deputy in Congress from Chachapoyas) has eaten off an ear of the *Maquisapa* (a stupid-looking black monkey) and the tail of another, called *Yanacmarchin.* Some savage unknown, though I strongly suspect my beautiful chiriclis, has bitten off the bill of the prettiest paroquet. There was a desperate battle between the friar and the chiriclis, in which one lost fur and the other feathers, and symptoms of warfare between a wild pig, called *Huangana,* and a *Coati,* or Mexican mongoose. The latter, however, fierce as he generally is, could not stand the gnash of the wild boar's teeth and prudently fled the fight. The life of the fowls is a state of continued strife and nothing has kept the peace except an affectionate and delicate Pinshi monkey (Humboldt's *Midas Leonina*) that sleeps upon my beard and hunts game in my moustachios.

We met two canoes that had come from near Quito by the Napo

and were bound to Tarapoto. This party embarked upon the Napo on the 3d of October. They told me that I could reach the mouth of the river Coca, which empties into the Napo, in two and a half months, from the mouth, but that I could go no further in my boat for want of water. There are very few Christianized towns upon the Napo and the rowers of these boats were a more savage-looking set than I had seen. I have met with a good many inhabitants of Quito in the Missions of the Huallaga, and many of the inhabitants are descendants of Quitenos. In fact, these Missions were formerly under the charge and direction of the Bishopric of Quito, and most of the Jesuits who first attempted the conversion of these Indians came from that quarter. There is a report now current in these parts that thirty Jesuits recently banished from New Granada have gone to Ecuador. They are said to have been well received, and have asked for the old Missions of the company, which has been granted to them as far as Ecuador has jurisdiction. This party from the Napo also reported that the governor (*Gefe Politico*) of the Ecuador territory of the Napo had left his place of residence and gone up the river for the purpose of supplying with laborers a French mining company that had recently arrived and was about to commence operations. It is generally thought that much gold is mixed with the sands of the Napo, but I think that the Moyobambinos would have it if it were there. They get a quill full of gold dust now and then from the Indians, but no regularly organized expedition for collecting it has been successful. It is said that the Indians of the Napo formerly paid their contributions to the government in gold dust, but now that they are relieved (as are all the Missions by express exception) from the burden of the contribution there is no more gold collected.

Fearful of going to the right of Iquitos Island, and thus passing the town, I passed to the left of some islands, and in running between the one just above Iquitos Island and the left bank of the river, the boat grounded near the middle of the passage, which was one hundred and fifty yards broad, and came near rolling over from the velocity of the current. We hauled over to the left bank and passed close along it in forty-two feet water. At half-past 9 P.M. we arrived at Iquitos.

November 7. Iquitos is a fishing village of two hundred and twenty-seven inhabitants. A considerable part of them, to the number of ninety-eight, are whites and Mestizos of San Borja who were driven from their homes a few years ago by the Huambisas of the Pastaza and Santiago. This occurred in 1841. In 1843, these same Indians murdered all the inhabitants of a village called Santa Teresa, situated on the upper Marañon, between the mouths of the rivers Santiago and Morona. My companion Ijurra was there soon after the occurrence. He gave the dead bodies burial and published, in his *Travels in Mainas,* a detailed account of the affair.

In October, 1843, Ijurra, with seventeen other young men of Moyobamba, formed a company for the purpose of washing for gold the sands of the Santiago. Furnished with arms by the prefecture, they recruited sixty-six Cocamillas of Laguna, armed with bows and arrows, as a light protecting force. They also engaged eighty-five of the Indians of Jeveros as laborers at the washings, and, after they started, were joined by four hundred and fifty of the people who had been expelled in 1841 from Santiago and Borja, desirous of recovering their homes and taking vengeance of the savages.

The party went by land to the port of Barranca, at the mouth of the river Cahuapanas, when they embarked to ascend the Amazon to the mouth of the Santiago. At Barranca they received intelligence of the massacre at Santa Teresa.

A Moyobambino, Canuto Acosta, fearing that the company would get all the gold, hastened on before. He met at Santa Teresa with a large party of Huambisas, who had come down the Santiago for the ostensible purpose of trade. Conversing with the curaca of the tribe, named Ambuscha, Acosta told him that a multitude of Christians were coming with arms in their hands to conquer and enslave his people. The curaca, turning the con-

132

versation, asked Acosta what he had in his packages. The reply was more foolish and wicked than the other speech; for, desirous to play upon the credulity of the Indian, or to overawe him, Acosta said that he had in his packages a great many epidemic diseases, with which he could kill the whole tribe of the Huambisas. It was his death warrant. The curaca plunged his spear into his body and gave a shrill whistle; his people, who were scattered about among the houses, commenced the massacre. They killed forty-seven men and carried off sixty women; some few persons escaped into the woods. The Indians spared two boys— one of seven and one of nine years—and set them adrift upon the Amazon on a raft, with a message to the gold-hunting company that they knew of their approach and were ready with the assistance of their friends the Paturos and Chinganos to meet and dispute with them the possession of the country. The raft was seen floating past Barranca and brought in.

The gold-seekers found no gold upon the borders of the Marañón; quarrelled; became afraid of the savages; broke up and abandoned their purpose before they reached the mouth of the Santiago. Ijurra and a few others then turned their attention to the collection of Peruvian bark. They spent two or three years in the woods, about the mouth of the Huallaga, gathered an enormous quantity and floated it down to Pará on immense rafts; Ijurra describes these as floating-houses with all the comforts and conveniences of a dwelling on shore.

When they arrived at Pará, the cargo was examined by chemists and said by them to be good. A mercantile house offered eighty thousand dollars for it. They refused the offer, chartered a vessel, and took the cargo to Liverpool where other chemists pronounced the fruit of years of labor to be utterly worthless.

To get back to more immediate matters, the village of Iquitos is situated on an elevated plain which is said to extend far back from the shores of the river. This is different from the situation of many towns upon the Amazon, most of which are built upon a hill, with a low, swampy country behind them. Cotton and

133

coffee-trees grow in the streets of the village, but no attention is paid to the cultivation of either. A small stream, said to be one of the mouths of the river Nanay, enters the Amazon just above the town.

We left Iquitos at half-past 9 A.M. The shores of the river just below are bold and of white clay; at a quarter to eleven we passed the main mouth of the Nanay, about one hundred and fifty yards broad. The depth of the Amazon at the junction of the two rivers is fifty feet; the current a mile and two-thirds the hour. After passing several small islands, where the river appeared two miles wide, it seemed to contract within its own banks to half a mile, immediately in front of a settlement of two or three houses, called Tinicuro, where I found no bottom at one hundred and eighty feet. At half-past five we arrived at Pucallpa, where we passed the night.

November 8. Pucallpa, or New Oran, is a small settlement of twenty houses and one hundred and eleven inhabitants, who formerly belonged to Oran, but who, finding their situation uncomfortable, removed and settled here. It is one of the most pleasantly situated places I have seen—on a moderate eminence, with green banks shelving to the river. The water is bold (twenty-five to thirty feet deep) close to the shore. Two islands—one above and one below the town, with a narrow opening in front—gave the place the appearance of a snug little harbor.

We bought at this place two of the great cranes of the river, called Tuyuyú. These were gray. Started at 4 A.M.; high white chalky banks just below Pucallpa. At nine we arrived at the mouth of the Napo. We found it two hundred yards broad and of a gentle current. The soundings across the mouth were thirty-five and forty feet. Stopped at Chorococha, a settlement of eighteen inhabitants, just below the mouth of the Napo. We found some of our Nauta friends here salting fish and got a capital breakfast from them.

November 9. We started at 5 A.M. and arrived at Pebas at 10 A.M. We found that the people of Pebas, under the direction of

134

Father Valdivia (my Nauta friend), were establishing a new town about a quarter of a mile up a stream called Ambiyacu, which enters into the Amazon two miles above Pebas. We pulled up this stream and found the good priest and the governor general busy in directing the felling of trees and building of houses. I determined to stay here for some time, for I was now getting so weak that I could scarcely climb the banks upon which the towns are situated. Father Valdivia received us with great cordiality and gave us quarters in a new house he was building for himself.

The new settlement had not yet a name, but the population already numbered three hundred and twenty-eight—almost all the people of Pebas having come over. The inhabitants are principally *Oregones,* or Big Ears, from the custom of introducing a bit of wood into a slit in the ear and gradually increasing the size of it until the lobe hangs upon the shoulder. They have, however, now discontinued the custom and I saw only a few old people thus deformed.

November 15. Ijurra and I went with the padre to visit his mission of San José of the Yaguas. This is a settlement of Yaguas Indians of two hundred and sixty inhabitants about ten miles in a N.E. direction from Ambiyacu. San José is reached by a path through the woods over a rather broken country. There were two or three rivulets, which have pebbly beds, to pass on the road, with black slate rock cropping out of the sides of the ravine—the first stones I have seen since leaving Chasuta. The soil is dark clay and deeper than I have seen it elsewhere on the river. Birds of a brilliant plumage occasionally flitted across our path and the woods were fragrant with aromatic odors.

The Yaguas received their priest in procession, with ringing of the church bell and music of drums. They conducted him, under little arches of palm branches stuck in the path, to a building that is used to house the padres, and politely left us to rest after the fatigue of the walk. These are the most thorough-looking savages in their general appearance and costume, though without anything savage in the expression of their countenances, which is

135

vacant and stupid. Their ordinary dress consists of a girdle of bark around the loins, with a bunch of fibres of another kind of bark, looking like a swab or mop, about a foot in length, hanging down from the girdle in front and rear. Similar, but smaller bunches, are hung around the neck and arms by a collar and bracelets of small beads. This is the every-day costume. On festivals they stain all their bodies a light brown, and on this ground they execute fantastic devices in red and blue. Long tail-feathers of the macaw are stuck in the armlets, reaching above the shoulders, and a chaplet, made of white feathers from the wings of a smaller bird, is worn around the head. This generally completes the costume, though I did see one dandy who had glued short white feathers all over his face, leaving only the eyes, nose, and mouth exposed. The curaca, or headman, and some one or two of the Varayos wore frocks and trousers; but I was told they had the national costume underneath these. The dress of the women is a yard or two of cotton cloth rolled around the hips.

Their houses are peculiar. Very long, slender poles are stuck in the ground opposite each other about thirty feet apart; their ends are brought together at the top, forming a Gothic arch about twenty feet high. Similar poles, of different lengths, are planted in front of the openings of the arch, and their ends are brought down and lashed to the top and sides of the openings. They are secured by cross-poles, inside and out, and the whole is thickly thatched to the ground, leaving two or three apertures for entrance. The house looks, on the outside, like a gigantic beehive. On the inside, small cabins of cane are built at intervals around the walls, each one of which is the sleeping-room of a family. Four or five families generally occupy one house and the middle space is used in common. This is never cleaned, nor even levelled, and is littered with all manner of abominations. There is a puddle of water before each door; by virtue of the construction of the house, the rain, both from the heavens and the roof, pours directly into the everlasting pool.

After evening service, the Indians went off to their houses to commence the festival. They kept the drums going all night and until 10 o'clock next morning, when they came in a body to conduct us to mass. Most of them were the worse for their night's debauch and sat upon the ground in a listless and stupid manner, occasionally talking and laughing with each other and little edified, I fear, by the sacred ceremony.

I was both depressed and annoyed at the poverty of the church, and determined, if I ever went back, that I would appeal to the Roman Catholics of the United States for donations. The priestly vestments were in rags. The lavatory was a gourd, a little earthen pitcher, and a jack towel of cotton. It grieved me to see the host taken from a shaving box and the sanctified wine poured from a vinegar cruet.

After mass and a procession, the Indians went back with us to the convento and entertained us with music whilst we breakfasted. It was well that the drums were small, or we should have been fairly deafened. There were six of them and they were beaten without intermission. One fellow dropped off to sleep, but we gained nothing by this, for his neighbor beat his drum for him. Nearly the whole male population were crowded into the structure where we were housed. The breakfast was furnished by the Indians, each family contributing its share. The women were proud of their dishes and seemed gratified when we partook of them. They continued their frolic all day and night.

On Monday we visited the houses of the Indians to see what curiosities we could get. We found the men stretched in their hammocks, sleeping off the effects of the celebration, and the patient, much-enduring women at work twisting chambira for hammocks, or preparing yuccas or plantains to make drink for their lords. We could get nothing except a hammock or two and some twisted chambira to make me a sounding line. The Indians had hidden their hammocks and we had to go searching for them. The reason for this was that most of them owe the padre, and the paying of debts seems as distasteful to the savage man as to the civilized.

137

The hammocks we acquired were very coarse ones, made of the fibres of the budding top of a species of palm. The tree is very hard and is defended with long sharp thorns, so that it is a labor of a day to cut a top, split the leaves into strips of convenient breadth, and strip off the fibres, which are the outer covering of the leaves. The stripping process is done very dexterously with the finger and thumb. A top of ordinary size yields about half a pound of fibres, and when it is reflected that these fibres have to be twisted, a portion of them dyed, and then woven into hammocks of three or four pounds weight, it will be seen that the Indian is very poorly paid for his labor when he receives for a hammock twelve and a half cents in silver, or twenty-five cents in *efectos*.

The women twist the thread with great dexterity. They sit on the ground, and taking two threads, which consist of a number of minute fibres, between the finger and thumb of the left hand, they lay them, separated a little, on the right thigh. A roll of them down the thigh, under the right hand, twists each thread; then, with a scarcely perceptible motion of the hand, the worker brings the two together, and a roll up the thigh makes the cord. A woman will twist fifty fathoms about the size of ordinary twine in a day.

The history of the settlement of this place is remarkable, in that it shows the attachment of the Indians to their pastor and their church. Some years ago Padre José de la Rosa Alva had established a mission at a settlement of the Yaguas, about two days' journey to the northward and eastward of the present station, which he called Santa Maria and where he generally resided. Business took him to Pebas and unexpectedly detained him there for fifteen days. The Indians, finding he did not return, reasoned with themselves and said, "Our father has left us; let us go to him." Whereupon they gathered together the personal property the priest had left; shouldered the church utensils and furniture, even to the doors; set fire to their houses, and joined the padre in Pebas. He directed them to the present sta-

138

tion, where they built their houses and established themselves. Our little padre also has considerable influence over them, though, when he will not accede to all their demands, they contrast his conduct with that of Father Rosa, call him mean, get sulky, and won't go to mass.

November 18. Returned to Echenique; the walk occupied three hours without stopping. Although the Orejones have left off some of their savage customs and are becoming more civilized, they are still sufficiently barbarous to permit their women to do most of the work. I saw twenty of the lazy rascals loitering about, while the same number of women were fetching earth and water, trampling it into mud, and plastering walls with it. I also saw the women cleaning up and carrying away the weeds and bushes of the town; most of them, too, with infants hanging to their backs. These marry very young. I saw some, whom I took to be children, with babies that I was told were their own.

The mosquitoes are very troublesome here. I have to write my journal under a mosquito curtain, and while I am engaged in skinning birds it is necessary to have an Indian with a fan to keep the stinging insects off; even this does not succeed, and my face and hands are frequently quite bloody, where my Indian has to kill them with his fingers. The Indians bring me a number of very beautiful birds every evening, and I have my hands full, even with the occasional assistance of Arebalo and the padre's servant.

We have increased our stock of animals largely at this place. They now number thirteen monkeys, a mongoose, and a wild pig (the Mexican peccary), and thirty-one birds. I bought a young monkey of an Indian woman to-day. It had coarse gray and white hair; that on the top of its head was stiff, like the quills of the porcupine, and smoothed down in front as if it had been combed. I offered the little fellow some plantain but he would not eat; the woman then took him and put him to her breast, where he sucked away manfully and with great gusto. She weaned him in a week so that he would eat plantain mashed up and put into his mouth in small bits, but the little beast died of mortification because I would not let him sleep with his arms around my neck.

November 24. Preparing for departure. Our boat, which had been very badly calked in Nauta, required re-calking. The tow, or filling, used is the inner bark of a tree called *machinapuro*, beaten and mashed into fibres. It answers very well and there is great abundance in the forest. Its cost is twelve and a half cents the mantada, or as much as an Indian can carry in his blanket. An Indian can gather and grind two mantadas in a day. Ten or twelve mantadas are required to calk such a boat as mine. The pitch of the country is said to be the deposit of an ant in the trees. I never saw it in its original state. It is gathered by the Indians, heated till soft, and made into the shape of wide, thin bricks. It is very indifferent. A better kind is made by mixing black wax with gum copal.

Father Valdivia, who is half Indian, entertained us most kindly. His aguadiente gave out and he occasionally regaled us with a glass of wine, bought for the church in Loreto. It is a weak white wine. I suppose I could not drink it at home, but here it seems very good. I find that this is the case with a great many things. The green plantains, roasted, which were at first an abomination to me, have now become a very good substitute for bread, and a roasted yucca is quite a treat. We have some small red-headed pan fish that are very fine; at my suggestion, the padre had two or three fried, added to his usual evening cup of chocolate. I look forward to this meal with considerable pleasure. I do not know if it arises from the fact of our seeing so few things that are good to eat, or from the freshness of the cocoa, but chocolate, which I could not touch before this, is now very palatable and refreshing. The bean is simply toasted and pulverized and the chocolate is made nearly as we make coffee. After supper, we—that is, the padre, the governor general, Ijurra, and I, provided with fans to keep off the mosquitoes—light our cigars, stretch ourselves at full length in a hammock, and pass an hour before bed-time in agreeable conversation.

We obtained from the Indians more of the poisonous milk of

140

the catao, and also the milk of a tree known as the cow-tree. This they drink when fresh. When brought to me in a calabash it had a foamy appearance, as if just drawn from the cow, and looked very rich and tempting. It coagulates very soon, however, and becomes as hard and tenacious as glue. The Indians make use of this property of it to eradicate their eyebrows. This is not so painful an operation as it would seem, for the Indians have never suffered the eyebrows to grow and become strong and the hair is only down, which is easily plucked up. When the milk coagulates, it expands, so that it forced the glass stopper out of the bottle I put it in, though sealed with pitch. We also got some of the almonds of the country, which I have not seen elsewhere. They are about the size, and have somewhat the appearance, of our common black walnut, with a single oblong kernel similar in taste to the Brazil nut.

November 26. We had much heavy rain for the last day or two. A number of persons were affected with catarrh and headache. The padre told me that half of the population were ill of it and that this always happens at the commencement of the rains. The disease is called *romadizo* and is like our influenza. Ijurra and I were both indisposed with rheumatic pains in the back of the neck and shoulders. I don't wonder at this, for we have slept all the time in a room just plastered with mud, and so damp that where my bedclothes came in contact with the wall they were quite wet, and the rain beat in upon my head and shoulders. My boots are covered with mould every morning and the guns get half full of water.

I gave the padre's servant, who was suffering very much from romadizo, fifteen grains of Dover's powder (Heaven knows if it were proper or not), and to the padre's sister, who has been suffering for some days with painful diarrhoea, forty drops of laudanum. The old lady was cured at once and said she had never met with so great a remedio. I left her a phial of it with directions for its use, telling her (at which she looked aghast) that it was a deadly poison. It is curious to see how entirely ignorant the best-informed people out here are concerning the properties of medicines. Most of them do not know the names, much less the effects, of even such common drugs as calomel and opium.

We sailed from Echenique at half-past 1 P.M. Father Valdivia, who is musical, but chanted the mass in a falsetto that would be very difficult to distinguish at a little distance from the rattling of a tin pan, commissioned me to bring him out (should I ever return) a small piano and a French horn, which he would pay for in salt fish and sarsaparilla. I cannot refrain from expressing my grateful thanks to my friends—the well-informed and gentlemanly Arebalo and the pious, simple-minded, single-hearted little Indian priest of Pebas. We arrived at Cochiquinas (twenty-five miles distant) at half-past 8 P.M.

CHAPTER X

*   *   *

Cochiquinas, or New Cochiquinas, is a miserable fishing village
of two hundred and forty inhabitants, though at this time there
did not appear to be forty in the village, most of them being absent
fishing and seeking a livelihood. Old Cochiquinas is four miles
further down the river and seems a far better situation; the people there were afraid of the attacks of the savages of the Yavari
and moved up to this place.

The old town, to which we dropped down for our breakfast, has
one hundred and twenty inhabitants, of which twenty-five are
white and the rest Indians of the Yavari, called Marubos. These
are dressed with even more simplicity than the Yaguas, dispens-
ing with the mop behind. They have small, curly moustaches and
beards, are darker than the other Indians, and do nothing but
hunt for their living.

The governor treated us very civilly and gave us a good breakfast of soup, chickens, rice, and eggs, with milk just taken from
the cow. What a luxury! I saw before his door a large canoe filled
with unshelled rice of very good quality. The governor told us
that rice grew very well and gave about forty-fold in five months.
He seemed a very gay and good-tempered young person, with a
fine family of a wife and eleven remarkably handsome children—
some born in lawful wedlock, others natural—but all cared for

143

alike and brought up together. I had the impertinence to ask him how he supported so many people. He said that the forest and the river yielded abundantly and that he occasionally made an expedition to the Napo, collecting enough sarsaparilla to buy clothes and luxuries for his family. The Napo, he says, is very full of sand-banks and that twenty days from its mouth the men have to get overboard and drag the canoes.

November 28. From Cochiquinas to Camucheros is fifty miles. This place has only a population of four families, recently settled there, who have cleared away a small portion of the forest and commenced their plantations of yuccas, maize, and rice. Just below Camucheros we had apparently all the width of the river in view—about a mile broad. I was surprised to find, near the middle of it, only thirty feet of water. The velocity of the current was two and a quarter miles the hour. We arrived at Moromoroté at a quarter past 6 P.M. (distance fifteen miles). This consists of one house of Christianized Indians. We could hear the sound of their music and sent them word that we wanted to buy animals and food from them. They came to see us after night, but were drunk and had nothing to sell.

November 29. We passed to-day a number of small islands. Between one of them and the right bank, where the river was at least a quarter of a mile wide, we saw many trees grounded. At 9 A.M., after a journey of twenty miles, we entered the caño of Caballo Cocha (Horse Lake). It is about eighty yards wide. The water is clear and makes an agreeable contrast with the muddy waters of the Amazon.

The village is situated on the caño, about a mile and a half from the entrance and at the same distance from the lake. It contains two hundred and seventy-five inhabitants, mostly Ticunas Indians. These are darker than the generality of Indians of the Marañon, though not so dark as the Marubos, which frees them from the Negroid look that these last have. Their houses are generally plastered with mud inside and are far neater-looking and more comfortable than any of the other Indian residences that

144

I have seen. I suspect, however, that this is entirely owing to the activity and energy of the priest, Father Flores, who seems to have them in excellent order. They are now building a church for him, which, when finished, will be the finest in the region.

The men are all decently clad in frocks and trousers. The women, besides the usual roll of cotton cloth around the loins, wear a short tunic covering the breast. I think that Father Flores, though he wants the honest simplicity and kindness of heart of Valdivia and the noble patience, magnanimity, and gentleness of dear Father Calvo, is a better man for the Indians, and more successful in their management, than either of the others. He does not seem to care about their coming to church, for there was not an Indian at mass Sunday morning (though the padre did give us a little homily on the importance of attending worship), but he sees that they keep themselves and their houses clean and the streets of the village in order. I saw none of the abominable drinking and dancing with which the other Indians invariably wind up the Sunday.

It is very dangerous to bathe in the caño on account of the alligators. Not long before my arrival, a woman, bathing after nightfall in company with her husband, was seized and carried off by one of those monsters. She was not even in the caño, but was sitting on the bank, pouring water over her head with a gourd, when the reptile crawled from behind a log where it had been lying and carried her off in its mouth, though struck several heavy blows with a stick by the unfortunate husband. The padre next morning declared war upon the alligators and had the Indians out with their harpoons and lances to destroy them. They killed a number and thought it remarkable that the first they killed should have parts of the woman yet undigested in its stomach. I think it probable that a good many alligators had a bite.

Padre Flores, as is usual with the padres, gave us a room in his house and seats at his table. I admired a very old-looking silver spoon that he had on the table and which Ijurra judged to be of

145

the date of Ferdinand and Isabella, from the armed figures and lion's head upon the handle; whereupon our host, with the courtesy that belongs to his race, insisted upon my accepting it. I was glad to have it in my power to acknowledge the civility by pressing upon the padre a set of tumblers neatly put up in a morocco case, which had been given me as a parting gift by one of the officers aboard the *Vandalia*.

After dark he proposed that we should go out and see some of the incantations of the Indians for the cure of the sick. We heard music at a distance and approached a large house whence it proceeded, in which the padre said there was almost always some one sick. We listened at the door, which was closed. There seemed to be a number of persons singing inside. I was almost enchanted myself. I never heard such tones and think that even instrumental music could not be made to equal them. I have frequently been astonished at the power of the Indians to mock animals, but I had heard nothing like this before. The tones were so low, so faint, so guttural, and at the same time so sweet and clear, that I could scarcely believe they came from human throats; they truly seemed fitting sounds in which to address spirits of another world.

Ijurra, with his usual audacity, pushed open the door and proposed to enter. The noise we made in opening the door caused a hasty retreat of some persons, whom we could hear and partly see. When we entered, we found but two Indians—an old man and a young one—sitting on the floor engaged in chewing tobacco and spitting in an earthen pot before them. The young man turned his face to the wall with a sullen look, and although the old man smiled, it was with a smile that had no mirth or satisfaction in it, and showed plainly that he was annoyed.

The hut, a large one, appeared larger in the gloom. There was a light burning in the farther end of it which looked to be a mile off. Ijurra strode the distance and found it to be twenty-four paces. There was a number of hammocks slung one above the other between the posts that supported the roof and all seemed occupied. In one corner of the house was built a small partition of

146

cane, in which I understood was confined a young girl, who was probably looking at us with curious eyes, but whom we could not see. I had been told before that it was the custom among most of the Indians of the Montaña to shut up a girl when she entered into the period of womanhood, until the family could raise the means for a feast, when everybody is invited. All hands then get drunk and the maiden is produced with much ceremony and declared a woman of the tribe whose hand may be sought in marriage. The confinements sometimes last several months. The Indians do not hurry themselves in making their preparations, but are ready when the yuccas are gathered, the masato made, and there is a sufficient quantity of dried monkey in the house; so that it sometimes happens that when the poor girl is brought out she is nearly white. It is said that she frequently conceals her situation from her family, preferring a sound beating, when time betrays her, to this dreary imprisonment.

December 1. I lost my beautiful and valued chiriclis, which died of the cold. It was put to bed as usual under the wash-basin, but the basin was not put under shelter, and it rained heavily all night. I was surprised at the delicacy of feeling shown by my Indian boatman on the occasion. They knew how much I was attached to the bird, and, instead of tossing the carcass overboard, as they would have done with that of any other animal that I had, one of them brought it into my room before I was awake and laid it decently, and with care, on a table at my bedside. I felt the loss very sensibly—first, because it was a present from good Father Calvo, upon whose head and shoulder I had so often seen it perched, and, secondly, on account of the bird itself. It was beautiful, gentle, and affectionate, and so gallant that I called it my Mohawk chief. I have seen it take the food, unresisted, out of the mouths of the parrots and macaws many times its size by the mere reputation of its valor, and it waged many a desperate battle with the monkeys. Its triumphant song when it had vanquished an adversary was most amusing. It was very pleasant, as the cool of night came on, to find it, with beak

147

and claws, climbing up the leg of my trousers until it arrived at the opening of my shirt, and to hear its low note of satisfaction as it entered and stowed itself snugly away in my armpit. It was as sensible of caresses, and as jealous, as a favorite; I could never notice my little Pinshi monkey in its sight that it did not fly at it and drive it off.

This bird is the *psit melanocephalus* of Linneus. It is about the size of a robin, has black legs, yellow thighs, a spotted white breast, orange neck and head, and a brilliant green back and wings. There is another species of the same bird in Brazil. It is there called *periquito,* and differs from this in having the feathers on the top of the head black, so as to have the appearance of wearing a cowl.

I noticed growing about the houses of the village a couple of shrubs, six or eight feet high, called, respectively, *yanapanga* and *pucapanga.* From the leaves of the first is made a black dye, and from those of the second a rich scarlet one. I surmised that a dye, like the indigo of commerce, though of course of different color, might be made of these leaves, and when I arrived in Brazil I found that the Indians there were in the habit of making a scarlet powder of the pucapanga, called carajurú, quite equal, in brilliancy of color, to the dye of the cochineal. I believe that efforts have been made to introduce this dye into commerce and I do not know why they have failed.

December 2. Much rain during the night. Sailed from Caballo Cocha at half-past 2 P.M. Ijurra liked the appearance of things so much at this place that he determined, when he should leave me, to return to it and clear land for a plantation.

I lost my sounding-lead soon after starting and had no soundings to Loreto where we arrived at half-past 7 P.M. (twenty miles). Loreto is situated on an eminence on the left bank, having a large island in front. The river is three-fourths of a mile wide and has one hundred and two feet of depth in mid-stream with three miles the hour of current. The soil is a light-colored, tenacious clay, which, in the time of the rains, makes walking almost impossible,

148

particularly as there are a number of cattle and hogs running about the village and trampling the clay into mire.

There are three mercantile houses in Loreto, all owned by Portuguese. They do a business of about ten thousand dollars a year. That much in goods, that is, from above and below, passes through their hands. I saw a schooner-rigged boat lying alongside the bank. She was about forty feet long and seven broad. The houses at Loreto are better built, and better furnished, than those of the towns on the river above. We are approaching civilization. The population of Loreto is two hundred and fifty, made up of Brazilians, mulattoes, Negroes, and a few Ticunas Indians. It is the frontier post of Peru. There are a few miles of neutral territory between it and Tabatinga, the frontier of Brazil.

December 4. We left Loreto at half-past 6 A.M., with a cold wind from the northward and eastward, and rain. Thermometer, 76°. It seems strange to call the weather cold with the thermometer at 76°, but I really was very uncomfortable with it, and the monkeys seemed nearly frozen.

I estimate the length of the neutral territory, by the windings of the river, at twenty miles.

Since I purchased a boat at Nauta, I had worn an American flag over it. I had been told that I probably would not be allowed to wear it in the waters of Brazil. But when the boat was descried at Tabatinga the Brazilian flag was hoisted at that place, and when I landed, which I did dressed in uniform, I was received by the commandant, also in uniform, to whom I immediately presented my Brazilian passport, of which the following is a translation:

I, Sergio Teixeira de Macedo, of the Council of his Majesty, the Emperor of Brazil, his Envoy Extraordinary and Minister Plenipotentiary near the United States of America, Officer of the Imperial Order of the Rose, Grand Cross of that of Christ, and *Commendador* of various Foreign Orders, &c., &c.:

Make known to all who shall see this passport, that *William L. Herndon,* lieutenant of the navy of the United States, and *Lardner Gibbon,* passed midshipman of the same, prosecute a voyage for the purpose of making geographical and scientific explorations from the republic of Peru, by the river Amazon and adjacent parts, to its mouth; and I charge all the authorities, civil, military, and political, of the empire, through whose districts they may have occasion to pass, that they place no obstacle in the way, as well of them as of the *persons of their company;* but rather that they shall lend them all the facilities they may need, for the better prosecution of their enterprise.

For which purpose I have caused to be issued this passport, which I sign and seal with the seal of my arms.

Imperial Legation of Brazil, in Washington,

February 27, 1851

(Seal)   SERGIO TEIXEIRA DE MACEDO

By order of his Excellency:

ANTO. ZE DUARDE GONDIM

Secretary of Legation

As soon as my rank was ascertained (which appeared to be that of a captain in the Brazilian army), I was saluted with seven guns. The commandant used much stately ceremony towards me, but never left me a moment to myself until he saw me safely in bed on board my boat. I did not know, at first, whether this was polite attention or a watch upon me, but I think it was the latter. Upon giving him the slip and walking over towards the old fort, he joined me within five minutes. When we returned to his house, he brought a dictionary and, pointing with a cunning expression to the verb *traçar* (to draw), asked me to read it. I did so, and handed the book back to him, when he pointed out to me the verb *delinhar.* I was a little fretted and told him that I had no intention of making any drawings whatever and had merely intended to take a walk. He treated me with great civility and entertained me at his table, giving me roast-beef, which was a great treat.

It was quite pleasant, after coming from the Peruvian villages, which are all nearly hidden in the woods, to see that Tabatinga had the forest cleared away from about it for a space of forty or fifty acres and had a grove of orange-trees in its midst, though they were now old and past bearing. There are few houses to be seen, for those of the Ticunas are still in the woods. Those that are visible are the soldiers' quarters and the residences of a few whites that live here—white, however, only in contradistinction to the Indian. I think the only pure white man in the place was a Frenchman, who has resided a long time in Brazil and has a large Brazilian family. The post is garrisoned by twenty soldiers, commanded by *O Illustrissimo Senhor Tenente José Virisimo dos Santos Lima,* a cadet, a sergeant, and a corporal. The population of Tabatinga is about two hundred, mostly Indians of the Ticuna tribe. It is well situated for a frontier post, having all the river in front, only half a mile wide, and commanded from the fort by the longest range of cannon-shot. The fort is at present in ruins and the artillery consists of two long brass twelve-pounder field-guns.

I did not hoist my flag again and the commandant seemed pleased. He said that it might give offence down the river and told me that Count Castelnau, who had passed here some years before, borrowed a Brazilian flag from him and used that. He also earnestly insisted that I should take his boat in lieu of my own, which he said was not large enough for the navigation of the lower part of the Amazon. I declined for a long time, but finding that he was very earnest about it, and embarrassed between his desire to comply with the request of the Brazilian minister at Washington, contained in my passport—"that Brazilian authorities should facilitate me in my voyage, and put no obstacle in my way"—and the requirements of the law of the empire forbidding foreign vessels to navigate its interior waters, I accepted his proposition and exchanged boats; thus enabling him to say, in a frontier passport which he issued to me, that I was descending the river in Brazilian vessels.

He desired me to leave his boat at Barra, telling me he had no doubt but that the government authorities there would furnish me with a better one. I told him very plainly that I had doubts of that and that I might have to take his boat on to Pará. I was correct in my doubts, for, so far from the government authorities at Barra having a boat to place at my disposal, they borrowed mine and sent it up the river for a load of wood for building purposes. The commandant at Tabatinga, I was told, compelled the circus company that preceded me to abandon their Peruvian-built raft and construct another of the wood of the Brazilian forests.

December 5. We were employed in fitting up the new boat, to which the commandant gave his personal attention. I asked him to give me some more peons. He said, "Certainly," sent out a guard of soldiers, pressed five Tucunas into service, put them in the guard house till I was ready to start, and then marched them down to the boat with a Negro soldier to take charge of them. The commandant gave me all the beasts and birds he had, a demijohn of red wine, salt fish, and farinha for my men, and in short loaded me with kindness and civility. I had already parted with all the personal belongings that I thought would be valuable and acceptable to my friends on the route, and could only make a show of acknowledgment by giving him, in return, a dozen ropes of tobacco—an article which happened at this time to be scarce and valuable.

December 6. We embarked at half-past 1 P.M., accompanied by the commandant, the cadet, and the Frenchman, Jeronymo Fort, who had been kind enough to place his house at Egas at my disposal. Ijurra had privately got all the guns and pistols ready and we received the commandant with a salute of, I should think, at least one hundred guns—Ijurra did not leave off shooting for half an hour. They dropped down the river with us till 5 P.M., when, taking a parting cup with the commandant to the health of his Majesty the Emperor, we embraced and parted.

December 7. The river now has lost its name of Marañon, and, since the junction of the Yavari, is called Solimões. It is here a mile and a half wide, sixty-six feet deep in the middle, and has a current of two miles and three-quarters per hour. The small boat in which we carry our animals did not stop with us last night, but passed on without being noticed. She had all our fowls and turtles, so that our breakfast this morning consisted of boiled rice. We drifted with the tide all night, stopping for an hour in consequence of a severe squall of wind and rain from the eastward.

December 8. Rainy morning. We arrived at San Paulo at 10 A.M. This village is on a hill two or three hundred feet above the present level of the river—the highest situation I have yet seen. The population is three hundred and fifty, made up of thirty whites, and the rest Tucunas and Juries Indians. The commandant is the Lieutenant Don José Patricio de Santa Ana. He gave us a good breakfast and some statistics.

December 9. At half-past 8 A.M. we arrived at Maturá, a settlement of four or five huts (with only one occupied) on a muddy bank. Its distance from San Paulo is fifty miles. The shores of the river are generally low, though there are reaches where its banks are forty or fifty feet high, commonly of white or red clay. There is much colored earth on the banks of the river—red, yellow, and white—which some people use to plaster the inside of their houses.

At half-past four we entered the mouth of the Ica, or Putumayo, fifteen miles from Maturá. This is a fine-looking river, half a mile broad at the mouth, and opening into an estuary (formed by the left bank of the Amazon and islands on the right hand) of a mile in width. San Antonio is a village about two miles below the mouth of the Ica. It is a collection of four or five houses of Brazilians and a few Indian huts. The people seemed mad for tobacco and begged me earnestly to sell them some. I told them I would not sell for money, but I was willing to exchange for things to eat, or for rare birds and beasts. They ransacked the town, but could only raise five fowls, half a dozen eggs, two small turtles, and three bunches of plantains. They had no animals but such as I already had, and I only bought a macaw and a *pavoncito,*

153

or little peacock. The little tobacco I gave for these things, however, was not enough to give everybody a smoke and they implored me to sell them some for money. They came to the canoe after night and showed so strong a desire to have it that I feared they would rob me. Finding me inexorable, they went off abusing me, which excited the wrath of Ijurra to a high pitch. Our stock of tobacco, which we had bought in Nauta, was now very much reduced. We had used it, during our voyage on the Ucayali, to purchase food and curiosities, and to give to the peons, who were not satisfied or contented unless they had an occasional smoke. We also had been liberal with it to governors and curates who had been civil to us, and now we had barely enough for our own use to last us to Barra.

December 10. Between San Antonio and Tunantins we met the governor of San Antonio, a military-looking white man, returning with his wife and children from a visit to Tunantins. I showed him my passport, which he asked for, and we interchanged civilities and presents; he giving me wild bird and water-melons, I making him a present of tobacco and a tinder-box. The species of bird he gave me is called, in Brazil, *Marianita*. This one took a singular disease by which it lost the use of its legs—hopped about for some days on the knee-joints, with the leg and foot turned upwards in front, and then died. At twenty miles from San Antonio we entered the mouth of the Tunantins river, where there is a village prettily situated on a slight green eminence on the left bank. One sees very few Indians in the Portuguese villages. They seem to live apart in the woods, and are, I think, gradually disappearing. They are used as beasts of burden and are thought no further of.

December 11. We stopped at a *factoria* on the left bank, sixty-five miles from Tunantins, where people were making manteiga.* The effect of mirage was here very remarkable. When within a mile or two of the factoria, I thought I saw quite a large town

* A kind of oil made from turtle eggs. The author describes the process a few paragraphs below. *H.B.*

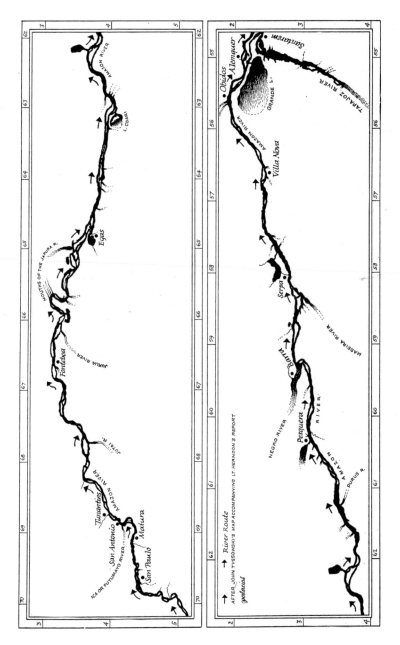

River Route

AFTER JOHN TYSSOWSKI'S MAP ACCOMPANYING LT. HERNDON'S REPORT

with houses of two or three stories, built of stone and brick, and large heaps of white stone lying about in several places. There was a vessel lying off the town that I was satisfied was a large man-of-war, but upon drawing near my three-story houses dwindled to the smallest palm huts, my heaps of building stones to piles of eggshells, and my man-of-war to a schooner of thirty tons.

The season for making manteiga on the Amazon generally ends by the first of November, but the rise of the river this year has been unusually late. The people are still collecting the eggs, though they all have young turtles in them.

A commandant, with soldiers, is appointed every year by some provincial or municipal authority to take care of the beaches, prevent disorder, and administer justice. Sentinels are placed at the beginning of August, when the turtles commence depositing their eggs, and are withdrawn when the beach is exhausted. They see that no one wantonly interferes with the turtles or destroys the eggs.

The process of making manteiga is very disgusting. The eggs, though they be rotten and offensive, are collected, thrown into a canoe, and trodden to a mass with the feet. The shells and young turtles are thrown out. Water is poured on and the residue is left to stand in the sun for several days. The oil, rising to the top, is skimmed off and boiled in large copper boilers. It is then put in earthen pots of about forty-five pounds weight. Each pot of oil is worth one dollar and thirty cents on the beach, and in Pará usually sells at from two and a half to three dollars.

A turtle averages eighty eggs; forty turtles will give a pot. Twenty-five men will make two hundred pots in twelve days. The beaches of the Amazon and tributaries yield from five to six thousand pots annually. The empty pot costs twelve and a half cents in Pará. Prolific as they are, I think the turtle is even now diminishing in number on the Amazon. Vast numbers of the young are eaten by the Indians, who take them by the time they are able to crawl and when they do not measure more than an inch in diameter, boil them, and eat them as a delicacy. One Indian will devour two dozen of these three or four times a day. The birds also pick up a great number of them as they crawl from their nest to the water. I imagine the fish, too, make them pay toll as they pass.

This factoria is a small one and will give but two or three hundred pots. One requires a good stomach to be able to eat his breakfast at one of these places. The stench is almost intolerable. The beach is covered with greedy and disgusting-looking buzzards, and the surface of the water dotted with the humps of the deadly alligator.

The Ticunas whom I brought with me from Tabatinga are even more lazy and careless than the Sarayaquinos. I fancied that it was because they were forced into the service and did not think that they would be paid; so I gave each one, as a gratuity, a knife, a pair of scissors, and a small mirror; but they were no better afterwards than before. Poor fellows! They have been abused and maltreated so long that they are now insensible even to kindness. The Negro soldier who was sent along, either as a pilot or to govern the Ticunas, or as a watch upon me, is drunken and worthless. He knows nothing of the river and I believe steals my liquor.

December 13. At 8 A.M. we entered a narrow arm of the river, sixty miles from the mouth of the Jutaí, that leads by Fonteboa. This canal separates the island of Cacao (on which much cocoa grows wild) from the mainland. There are eighty whites in Fonteboa. We met several traders at this place bound up and down the river. One named Guerrero, an intelligent-looking person, was going up with a cargo that I heard valued at twenty contos of reis (about ten thousand five hundred dollars). This was manifestly an exaggeration. His schooner, of some thirty-five tons burden, I think, could not carry the value of that sum in the heavy and bulky articles usually sent up the river. He had, however, a variety of articles. I bought some red wine and rum for stores, and Ijurra bought very good shoes and cotton stockings. This gentleman invited us to breakfast with him. His plates

158

and cups were of pewter and he seemed well equipped for travelling. Sailed at 3 P.M., and stopped for the night at half-past 6 P.M.

December 14. Misty morning. At ten entered the mouth of the Juruá, thirty-six miles from Fonteboa. It has half a mile of width at the mouth, but a mile up it seemed divided into two narrow channels by a large island. The Amazon is a mile and a quarter wide where the Juruá enters. We pulled half a mile up the stream. The water was clearer, though more yellow, than that of the Amazon. In running out the half mile that I had pulled up, which we did in mid-stream, the soundings deepened, as fast as I could heave the lead, from thirty-six to seventy-eight feet. The bottom was of white and black sand; temperature of the water 82°.

The Indians of the Juruá are Arauas and Catauxis, who are met with at eight days' journey up. Some of these are baptized Indians, but the Arauas are described as a treacherous people who frequently rob and murder the traders on the river. Two months further up are the Culinos and Nawas Infidels. Between these two was a nation called the Canamaris, but they have been nearly entirely destroyed by the Arauas. It is almost impossible to get an accurate idea of the number of the Indians, but I judge, from what I have seen and from the diversity of names of the tribes, that this is not great.

We breakfasted at the mouth of the river. After breakfast one of the Ticunas from Tabatinga was directed to take up one of the macaws that was walking on the beach and put it in the boat preparatory to a start. The man, in an angry and rude manner, took the bird up and tossed it into the boat, to the manifest danger of injuring it. I was standing in the larger boat close by and saw his insolent manner. I took up a paddle and beckoned him to come to me, but he walked sulkily up the beach. I thought it a good time to see whether, in the event of these surly fellows becoming mutinous, I could count upon my Sarayacu people, so I directed two of them to bring the Ticuna to me. They turned to obey, but slowly and evidently unwillingly, when my quick and passionate friend Ijurra sprang upon the Indian, and, taking him

159

by the collar, jerked him to where I was. I made great demonstrations with my paddle, though without the slightest idea of striking him (for I always shunned, with the utmost care, the rendering myself amenable to any of the tribunals or authorities of Brazil), and abused him in English, which I imagine answered quite as well as any other language but his own would have done. I think this little ''fracas'' had a happy effect upon all the Indians and they improved in cheerfulness and willingness to work afterwards. The Ticunas that I had with me, however, were far the laziest and most worthless people that I had hitherto had anything to do with. They were even too lazy to help to cook the provisions and when we stopped to breakfast they generally seated themselves on the thwarts of the boat, or on the sand of the beach, whilst the Sarayaquinos fetched the wood and made the fire. They were ready enough to eat when the breakfast was cooked. I couldn't stand this, when I observed that it was a customary thing, and accordingly caused the provisions issued to be divided between the two parties and told my Ticuna friends, ''No cook, no eat.''

December 15. We travelled till 11 P.M., for want of a beach to camp on, the men disliking to sleep in the woods on account of snakes.

December 16. Finding that I was on the southern bank, and having an opening between two islands abreast of me, I struck off to the eastward for the mouth of the Japurá. We ran through island passages till we reached it at 3 P.M., one hundred and five miles distant from the mouth of the Juruá.

The Indians of the Japurá are called Mirauas (a large tribe), Curitus, and Macus. The traveller reaches them in sixteen days from the mouth. The Macus have no houses, but wander in the woods, infest the river banks, and rob and kill when they can. (These are the fruits of the old Brazilian system of hunting Indians to make slaves of them.)

December 17. Started at 4 A.M. It was too dark to see the upper point of an island between us and the southern shore till we had passed it. We had to pull up for an hour against the current, so as to pass the head of this island and not fall below Egas. At half-past eight we entered a narrow channel between a small island and the right bank, which conducted us into the river of Teffé, about a mile inside of its mouth. The river at this point is one hundred and eighty yards broad; water clear and apparently deep. Just below Egas, where we arrived at half-past ten, it expands into a lake; or, rather, the lake here contracts into the river. The town is situated on a low point that stretches out into the lake and has a harbor on each side of it. On landing we showed our passports to the *sub-delegado,* an officer of the general government who has charge of the police of the district, and to the military commandant, and forthwith inducted ourselves into the house of M. Fort, our French friend of Tabatinga, who had placed it at our disposal.

CHAPTER XI

Egas—Lake Coari—Mouth of Rio Negro—Barra—Foreign Residents

* * *

Egas has a population of about eight hundred inhabitants and is the largest and most thriving place above Barra. It occupies an important position with regard to the trade of the river, being nearly midway between Barra and Loreto (the Peruvian frontier) and near the mouths of the great rivers Juruá, Japurá, and Teffé. There are now eight or ten commercial houses at Egas that drive a tolerably brisk trade between Peru and Pará, besides employing agents to go into the neighboring rivers and collect from the Indians the productions of the land and the water. Trade is carried on in schooners of between thirty and forty tons burden, which commonly average five months in the round trip between Egas and Pará, a distance of fourteen hundred and fifty miles. There are five such vessels engaged in this trade, each making two trips a year. Marcus Williams, a young American living at Barra, has one now off the mouth of the river, which has sent a boat in for provisions and stores.

There is much in this life of the *habilitado,* or person employed by the traders, to attract the attention of the active, energetic young men of our own country. It is true that he will encounter much hardship and some danger. These, however, are but stimulants to youth. It is also true that he will meet with a feeling of jealousy in the native towards the foreigner, but this feeling is principally directed towards the Portuguese, who are hard-working, keen, and clever and who, as a general rule, go to Brazil to make money and return home with it. This is their leading idea. It makes them frugal, even penurious, in their habits and indisposes them to make common cause with the natives of the country. Not so with the Italians, the French, the English, and the Americans whom I have met with in this country. I do not know more popular people than my friends Enrique Antonii, the Italian, and his associate Marcus Williams, the Yankee, who are established at Barra. Everywhere on the river I heard sounded the praises of my countryman. At Sarayacu, at Nauta, at Pebas, and at Egas, men said they wished to see him again and to trade with him. He himself told me that, though the trade on the river was attended with hardships, exposure, and privation, there was a certain charm attending the wild life and its freedom from restraint that would always prevent any desire on his part to return to his native country. I heard that he carried this feeling so far as to complain bitterly, when he visited Norris, the consul at Pará, of the restraints of society that compelled him to wear trousers at dinner.

December 25. We are very gay at Egas with Christmas time. The people keep it up with spirit and with a good deal of spirits, too, for I see a number of drunken people in the streets. I attended Midnight Mass last night. The church was filled with well-dressed people and with some very pretty, though dark-complexioned ladies. The congregation was devout, but I could not very well be so, on account of the music which was made by a hand-organ that wouldn't play. It gave a squeak and a grunt now and then, but there were parts of the music when nothing could be heard but the turning of the handle. There was also a display on the lake. A large, very well illuminated boat, moving about with rockets and music, and a long line of lights on logs and canoes anchored in the water, had a very pretty effect. Processions of singing Negroes, men and women, with music of tambourines and drums, paraded the streets all night.

December 26. I had requested the *commandante-militar* to furnish me with a few more Tapuios and he had promised to find me some. He now says there are none to be had, but I suspect he gave himself no trouble about it. Many persons go down the river with only two rowers and a steersman, and I having six, I have no doubt he thought that I had a sufficient number.

My Ticunas and the Negro soldier sent with them continue to give me a great deal of trouble—the soldier with his drunkenness and dishonesty and the Indians by their laziness and carelessness, suffering the boat to be injured for the want of care and permitting the escape and destruction of my animals and birds. It is as much as my patience and forbearance towards a suffering and ill-treated people can stand, to refrain from reporting them to the commandant, who would probably punish them with severity. Last night they broke the leg of one of my tuyuyús and an alligator carried off the other. I am told that these animals have killed three persons at this same place. I had bathed there twice a day until I heard this, but after that, although I knew that they only seize their prey at night, it was going too close to danger and I chose another place.

During our stay in Egas we are having our meals cooked by an old Negro woman who has charge of M. Fort's house, furnishing her with money to buy what she can. It is very difficult to get anything but turtle even here. I counted thirty-nine cattle grazing on the green slope before our door, yet neither for love or money could we get any beef and we had difficulty in getting a little milk for our coffee. We sent to Nogueyra for fowls and eggs, but without success. These are festival times and people want their little luxuries themselves, or are too busily engaged in frolicking to care about selling.

A local gentleman, Major Batalha, treated us with great kindness, sending us delicacies from his own table—the greatest of which was some well-made bread. We had not tasted any since leaving Huanuco—now five months. It was very welcome, of course. On Christmas day he sent us a pair of fine, large sponge-cakes. A piece of these, with a glass of tolerable ale, was a princely luncheon to us wayfarers who had lived so long on salt fish and farinha. It fairly made Ijurra grin with delight. We could always get a cup of very good chocolate by walking round to the Major's house and the only thing I had to find fault with was that he always received me alone. The Brazilians, as a general rule, do not like to introduce foreigners to their families, and their wives lead a monotonous and somewhat secluded life. An intelligent and spirited lady friend told me that the customs of her country confined and restrained her more than was agreeable, and said, with a smile, that she would not like to say how much she would be influenced in her choice of a husband by the hope that she would remove to another country, where she might see something, learn something, and be somebody.

December 28. We left Egas at half-past 2 P.M., in the rain. We seemed to have travelled just ahead of the rainy season and whenever we have stopped at any place for some days, the rains have caught up with us.

I now parted with my Sarayacu boatmen and very sorry I was to lose them. They were lazy enough, but were active and diligent compared with the stupid and listless Ticunas. They were always faithful and obedient, though somewhat careless. I believe that the regret at parting was mutual. Their earnest tone of voice and affectionate manner proclaimed their feeling, and a courtier, addressing his sovereign, would have envied the style in which old Andres bent his knee and kissed my hand and the tremulous tones, indicating deep feeling, with which he uttered the words *"Adios, mi patrón."* They are all going back to Sarayacu but one, who has engaged himself to Major Batalha. It is a curious thing that so many Peruvian Indians should be working in Brazil, but it shows that they are removed above the condition of savages, for, though worse treated in Brazil and deprived of the entire freedom of action they have in Peru, yet they can find work and are paid something for it. They acquire property, though it be nothing more than a painted wooden box with hinges and a lock to it (the thing they most covet), with a colored shirt and trousers to lock up in it and guard for feast-days. With such a box and contents, a hatchet, a short sabre, and red woolen cap, the Peruvian Indian returns home a rich and envied man, and others are induced to "go below" in hopes of similar fortune. They are frequently gone from their homes for years.

We entered the Amazon at 4 P.M. The mouth of the Teffé is three hundred yards wide and has thirty feet of depth and one mile per hour of current. This is an inconsiderable stream and may be ascended by canoes to near its sources in twenty days. In ten or twelve days' ascent, a branch called the Rio Gancho is reached, which communicates by a portage with the Juruá.

December 29. We drifted with the current, and a little paddling on the part of the crew, until 10 P.M., when we made fast to a tree on the right bank.

December 30. We started at 5 A.M. At 7 P.M. we arrived at the mouth of Lake Coari, one hundred and fifteen miles from Egas, and made fast to a schooner at anchor near the right bank. This schooner seemed to have no particular owner or captain, but to be manned by a company of adventurers. They were from Obidos, upwards of two months, and twenty-eight days from Barra, which place we expect to reach from here in five. They were travelling at their leisure, but complained much of the strength of the current and the want of strength of the easterly winds. I heard the same complaints at Egas, but I have found the winds quite fresh from the eastward and the current, compared with that above, slight.

December 31. We pulled into the Lake of Coari, but being told that it would take nearly all day to reach the village of Coari, and that it was an insignificant place where I would get neither supplies nor information, I decided not to go.

It may seem strange that just out of Egas I should need supplies, but all I could purchase there were half a dozen fowls, four turtles, and some farinha. Moreover, upon opening the baskets of farinha, it was found to be so old and sour that, though the Indians could eat it, I could not. Thus we had no bread, nor

166

even the substitute for it—plantains and farinha—and had to eat our meat with some dried peas that we fortunately found at Egas.

We pulled up the right bank of the lake about a mile and stopped at a little settlement of ten or twelve houses, but could get nothing. The people seemed afraid of us and shut their doors in our faces. The lieutenant, or principal man of the place, said that if we would give him money, he would send out and get us some fowls and plantains; but as he was a little drunk at this hour (seven in the morning), I would not trust him. We breakfasted and sailed at 11.

January 1, 1852. At 9 A.M. we had the easterly breeze so strong that we were compelled to keep close in shore to avoid the sea raised by it. Our heavy flat-bottomed boat rolls nearly gunwales under. Some of the Indians look alarmed, and Tomas, a new servant, is frightened from all propriety. He shouts to the men to make for the land and, seizing a paddle, makes one or two vigorous strokes, but fear takes away his strength, and he stretches himself on his face and yields to what appears his inevitable destiny. Ijurra is much scandalized at his cowardice and asks him what he would do if he got upon the sea.

January 2. The usual fresh easterly wind commenced at nine. The only time to make progress is at night. During the day the breeze is so fresh, and the sea so high, that very little is made. The wind usually subsides about 4 or 5 P.M. and concludes with a squall of wind and rain, leaving heavy-looking thunder-clouds in the southward and westward. The easterly wind often rises again and blows for a few hours at night.

January 3. We stopped to breakfast at nine, in company with a schooner bound up. She was three months from Pará and expected to be another month to Egas. Two others also passed us at a distance this morning. We arrived at the mouth of the Purus, one hundred and forty-five miles from Lake Coari. It is a fine-looking river, with moderately bold shores, masked by a great

167

quantity of bushes growing in the water. These bushes bore a great number of berries, which, when ripe, are purple and about the size of a fox-grape.

January 4. We travelled slowly all day on account of the fresh wind and sea. At 7 P.M. we stopped at the village of Pesquera, at the mouth of the Lake Manacapuru, forty-five miles from the mouth of the Purus. It has only three or four houses and is situated on a knee-cracking eminence of one hundred feet in height. The banks of the river are now losing the character of savage and desolate solitude that characterizes them above and begin to show signs of habitation and cultivation. We passed to-day several farms, with neatly framed and plastered houses, and schooner-rigged vessels lying off several of them.

January 5. At 3 A.M. we passed a rock in the stream called Calderon, or Big Pot, from the bubbling and boiling of the water over it when the river is full. We could hear the rush of the water against it, but could not see it on account of the darkness of the night. We stopped two hours to breakfast and then drifted with the current broadside to the wind (our six men being unable to keep the boat "head to it") until four, when the wind went down. At five we entered the Rio Negro. The right bank at the mouth is broken into islands and the black water of the Negro runs through the channels between these islands and alternates in patches (refusing to mingle) with the muddy waters of the Amazon. The entrance is broad and superb. It is far the largest tributary of the Amazon I have yet seen, and I estimate its width at the mouth at two miles.

There has been no exaggeration in the description of travellers regarding the blackness of its water. It well deserves the name of Rio Negro. When taken up in a tumbler, the water is a light-red color like a pale juniper water, and I should think it colored by some such berry. An object immersed in it has the color, though wanting the brilliancy, of red Bohemian glass. It may have been fancy, but I thought that the light cumuli that hung over the river were darker here than elsewhere. These dark, though peaceful-looking clouds, the setting sun, the glitter of the rising moon upon the sparkling ripples of the black water with its noble expanse gave us one of the fairest scenes that I have ever looked upon.

January 6. Started at 1 A.M. Moderate breeze from the eastward, blowing in squalls, with light rain. The left bank of the river is bold, and occasionally rocky. At 5 A.M. we arrived at Barra. My countryman, Mr. Marcus Williams, and Senhor Enrique Antonii, an Italian (merchants of the place), came on board to see me. Williams was fitting out for an expedition of six months up the river, but Antonii took me at once to his house and established me there snugly and comfortably. The greatest treat I met here, however, was a file of New York papers. They were not very recent, it is true, but still six months more recent than anything I had seen from home, and I read them with great interest and no small anxiety.

January 15. The town of Barra, capital of the province of Amazonas, is built on the left bank of the river about seven miles from its mouth. It is intersected by two or three ravines, containing more or less water, according to the state of the river, which are passed on tolerably constructed wooden bridges. The houses are generally of one story, though there are three or four of two, built of wood and adobe and roofed with tiles. The floors are also of tiles, and the walls are plastered with the colored earth which abounds on the banks of the Amazon. Every room has several hooks driven into the walls for the purpose of hanging hammocks. People find it more comfortable, on account of the heat, to sleep in hammocks, though I always suffered from cold and was obliged every night to wrap myself in a blanket.

I was surprised to find, before I left Barra, that provisions were getting very scarce. The supply of flour gave out, so that for some time there was no bread in the city, and beef was killed but once a fortnight. Even the staples of the country were difficult to procure, and I heard the President of the province, Senhor Aranha, say that he was desirous of recruiting some fifty or

169

sixty men to work on the new government buildings, but that he did not know where he could get enough salt fish and farinha to feed them with.

Williams is the only American resident in Barra. He was in partnership with an Irishman named Bradley, who died a few months ago of yellow fever in Pará. There had been another American in Barra a year ago. This was a deaf mute named Baker who was travelling in this country for a most unusual purpose. He carried with him tablets and a raised alphabet for the purpose of educating the deaf, dumb, and blind. He died on the 29th of April, 1850, at San Joachim, the frontier port of Brazil on the Rio Branco.

There are two English residents in Barra at the present time—Yates, a collector of shells and plants, and Hauxwell, a collector of bird-skins, which he prepares most beautifully. He uses the finest kind of shot and always carries in his pocket a white powder to stop the bleeding of the birds when shot. He admired some of my birds very much, and just a few days ago went with Williams up to Pebas, in Peru, where I procured most of them.

There is a little steamer in port, the chief engineer of which is a hard-headed, hot-tempered old Scotchman, who abuses the steamer in particular, and the service generally, in no measured terms. He desired to know if ever I saw such beef as was furnished to them and if we would give such beef to the dogs in my country. I told him that I thought he was fortunate to get beef at all, for that I had not seen any for a fortnight, and that if he had made such a voyage as I had recently, he would even find turtle and salt fish not such bad things. The steamer, though preserving a fair outside, is, I believe, very inefficient—the machinery wanting in power and being much out of order; indeed, so much so that on her downward passage she fairly broke down, and had to be towed into Pará. She, however, made the trip up in eighteen days, which, considering that the distance is full a thousand miles, that this was the first trip ever made up by steam, that the wood prepared for her had not had time to dry, and that there is nearly three-miles-an-hour current against her for about one-third of the distance, I do not consider a very bad run. The officers did not call to see me or invite me on board their vessel, though I met some of them at the evening parties given by the President.

Mr. Potter, a daguerreotypist and watchmaker, who came up in the steamer, and my good friend Enrique Antonii, the Italian, with his father-in-law, Senhor Brandâo, a Portuguese, make up the list of the foreigners of Barra as far as I know. Senhor Brandâo, however, has lived many years in the country, and has identified himself with it to the point where all his interests are Brazilian. He is a very intelligent man and I observe that he is consulted by the President and other officials in relation to the affairs of the new government. The province of which Barra is the capital has only been established this past year.

Speaking of persons, I should be derelict in the matter of gratitude if I fail to mention Donna Leocadia, the pretty, clever, and amiable wife of Enrique. She has exhibited great interest in my mission and has been always personally kind to myself. When our sunrise meal of coffee and buttered toast gave out, she would always manage to send me a tapioca custard, a bowl of caldo, or something nice and comfortable for a tired invalid. Unlike most Brazilian ladies, whenever her household duties permit, she always sits with the gentlemen, and takes an intelligent part in the conversation, expressing her desire to speak foreign languages and to visit foreign countries, that she might see and know what was in the world. A son was born to her whilst I was in the house, and we had become such friends that the young stranger was to be called *Luis* and I was to be *compadre* (godfather). But the church, very properly, would not give its sanction to the assumption by a heretic of the duties belonging to such a position.

Ijurra left me here and returned upstream with Williams. He laid out nearly all the money received for his services in such things as would best enable him to employ the Indians in the clearance of the forest and the establishment of a plantation, which he proposed to locate at Caballo Cocha, saying to me that he would have a grand crop of cotton and coffee ready against the arrival of my steamer—he fully expects me to come down with one.

Ijurra has all the qualities necessary for a successful struggle with the world save two—patience and judgment. He is brave, hardy, intelligent, and indefatigable. The river beach and a blanket are all that are necessary for him for a bed, and I believe that he could live on coffee and cigars. But his want of temper and discretion mars every scheme for prosperity. He spent a noble fortune, dug by his father from the *Mina del rey* at Cerro Pasco, in the political troubles of his country. He was appointed governor of the large and important province of Mainas, but, interfering with the elections, he was driven out. He then joined a party for the purpose of washing the sands of the Santiago for gold, but quarrels with his companions broke that up. With infinite labor he then collected an immense cargo of Peruvian bark, but, refusing eighty thousand dollars for it in Pará, he carried it to England where it was pronounced worthless and he lost the fruits of his enterprise and industry. He gave me infinite concern and some apprehension in the management of the Indians, but I shall never forget the untiring energy, the buoyancy of spirits, and the faithful loyalty that cheered my lonely journey and made the little Peruvian as dear to me as a brother.

CHAPTER XII

Departure from Barra—River Madeira—Serpa—Villa Nova—
Cocoa Plantations—Obidos—Santarem—Voyage to Pará

* * *

Having had my boat thoroughly repaired, calked, and well fitted with palm coverings, called *toldos,* I sailed from Barra on the eighteenth of February with a sort of Wandering-Jew feeling that I was destined to leave everybody behind and never to stop. The President had caused me to be furnished with six boatmen, but unwilling to dispossess himself at this time of a single working hand, he could not let them carry me below Santarem. The President is laboring in earnest for the good of the province and if anything is to be done for its improvement he will do it. He paid me every attention and kindness during my stay at Barra.

But to my host Antonii, the Italian, I am most indebted for attention and information. From his having been mentioned in some report as being at the head of trade at Barra sixteen years ago, I had fancied that I should find him an elderly man, but he is a handsome, gay, active fellow in the prime of life. His black hair is somewhat sprinkled with gray, but he tells me that this arises not from age but from the worry and vexation he has had in business. He is as agreeable as good sense, much information about the country, and warm, generous, open-hearted hospitality can make a man.

Mr. Potter, the daguerreotypist and watchmaker, sailed in company with me. About sixty miles below the mouth of the Rio Negro we stopped at the establishment of a Scotchman named McCulloch, situated on the left bank of the river. There is a very large island opposite, which reduces the river in front to about one hundred yards in width, so that the establishment seems to be situated on a creek. McCulloch, in partnership with Antonii, is establishing here a sugar plantation and a mill to grind the cane. He has dammed, at great cost of time and labor, a creek that connects a small lake with the river. He will only be able to grind about six months in the year, when the river is falling and the water runs from the lake into the river, but he proposes to grind with oxen when the river is rising. The difference between high- and low-water mark in the Amazon at this point is, by McCulloch's actual measurement, forty-two feet. He employs five or six hands, whom he pays a cruzado, or a quarter of a dollar each, per day. There is a much greater scarcity of workmen now than formerly. Antonii, who used always to have fifty in his employ, cannot now get more than ten.

McCulloch has already planted more than thirty acres of sugarcane on a hill eighty or one hundred feet above the present level of the river. It seems of tolerable quality, but much overrun with weeds on account of want of hands. I gave him a leaf from my experience and advised him to set fire to his field after every cutting. The soil is black and rich-looking, though light, and McCulloch supposes that in such soil his cane will not require replanting for twenty years. The cane is planted in December and is ready to cut in ten months.

This is the man who, in partnership with the Brazilian, built the saw-mill at Barra which was afterwards burned down. He sawed one hundred and thirty thousand feet the first year, but not more than half that quantity the second; in the third, by making a contract with Antonii, who was to furnish the wood and receive half the profits, he sawed eighty thousand. This plank is sold in Pará and the only wood sawed is the *cedro;* not that it is so valuable as other kinds, but because it is the only wood of any value that floats and thus can be brought to the mills. There are no roads or means of hauling timber through the forests. McCulloch told me that a young American, in Pará, offered to join

174

him in the erection of a saw-mill and to advance ten thousand dollars towards the enterprise. He said that he now thought he was unwise to refuse it, for with that sum he could have purchased a small steamer (besides building and fitting the mill) with which to cruise on the river, picking up the cedros and taking them to the mill.

These, incidentally, are not our cedars, but a tall, branching tree, with leaves more like our oak. There are two kinds, red and white, the former of which is most appreciated. Some of them grow to be of great size. On one occasion we made our boat fast to one that was floating on the river, which measured ninety-three feet in length from the swell of the roots to that of the first branches. It was nineteen feet in circumference just above the swell of the roots, which would probably have been eight feet from the ground when the tree was standing.

The distance hence to the mouth of the Madeira is about thirty miles. After passing the end of the long island, called Tamitari, that lies opposite McCulloch's, we had to cross the river, which there is about two miles wide. The shores are low on either hand and rather heavily wooded with small trees. I always felt some anxiety in crossing so large an expanse of water, where violent wind-storms are frequent occurrences, in such a boat as ours. Our men, with their light paddles, could not keep such a haystack as our clumsy, heavy boat either head to wind or before it, and she would, therefore, lie broadside to in the trough of the sea, rolling fearfully and threatening to swamp. I should have had sails fitted to her in Barra. At half-past 8 P.M. we made fast for the night to some bushes on the low, western bank of the Madeira.

The Madeira is by far the largest tributary of the Amazon. Once past its cascades, which are about four hundred and fifty miles from its mouth and occupy a space of three hundred and fifty miles in length, it is navigable for large vessels by its great tributaries—the Beni and Mamoré—into the heart of Bolivia, and by the Guaporé or Itenes quite through the rich Brazilian province of Matto Grosso. The Portuguese astronomers, charged with the investigation of the frontiers, estimate that it drains a surface equal to forty-four thousand square leagues.

The village of Serpa, where we arrived in the afternoon, is situated on the left bank of the Amazon, thirty miles below the mouth of the Madeira. It is a collection of mud-hovels of about two hundred souls, built upon a considerable eminence, broken and green with grass, that juts out into the river. We left Serpa at 6 P.M. and drifted all night. We are compelled to travel at night, for there is so much wind and sea during the day that we make no headway. We are frequently compelled to lay by, and are sometimes in danger of being swamped, even in the little nooks and bays where we stop. The most comfortable way of travelling is to make the boat fast to a floating tree, for this keeps the boat head on to the wind and sea and drags her along against these with the velocity of the current.

About fifteen miles above Villa Nova, which is one hundred and fifty miles below Serpa, a boat manned by soldiers pulled out from a hut on the shore and told us we must stop there until examined and despatched by the officer in charge, called inspector. I could not well pull back against the stream, for we had already passed the hut, so I sent word to the inspector that I had letters from the President and pulled inshore abreast of where I was. The inspector had the civility to come down to me and inspect my papers. He told me I was within four hours of Villa Nova, but I kept inshore for fear of squalls, and thus, in the darkness of night, pulled around the shore of a deep bay where there was little current and did not arrive for eight hours, passing the mouth of the small river Limão, about a mile and a half above Villa Nova, where we arrived at 2 A.M.

Villa Nova de Rainha is a long straggling village of single story mud-huts, situated in a little bend on the right bank of the Amazon. The people valued their fowls at fifty cents apiece. We thought them extortionate and would not buy; but we happened to arrive on fresh-beef day and got a soup-piece. These fresh-

176

Lith of P S Duval & Co Phila

CROSSING THE MOUTH OF THE MADEIRA RIVER   Brazil.

meat days are a week apart, though this is a cattle-producing country.

About a league below Villa Nova we passed the mouth of the river Ramos on the right. It has many small streams emptying into it in the interior and sends off canals, joining it with other rivers, one of which is the Madeira. Just below the mouth of the Ramos, quite a neatly rigged boat, carrying the Brazilian flag, put off from a house on shore and seemed desirous to communicate with us. She was so badly managed, however, that although there was a fine breeze directly ahead she could not catch us, though we were but drifting with the current. Finding that she could not come up with us, she put back, and a light canoe with a soldier in it soon overtook us. The soldier told me that this was another custom-house station and that I must pull back and show my clearance from the collector at Villa Nova. I was a good deal annoyed at this, for I thought the said collector, to whom I carried letters from the President, might have had the fore-thought to tell me about this station, so that I might have stopped there and saved the time and labor of pulling back. The soldier, seeing my vexation, told me that if I would merely pull inshore and wait, the inspector, who was then a few miles down the river, would soon be by on his way up and I could communicate with him there.

To do this even carried me some distance out of my way, but I smothered my annoyance, pulled in, and had the good luck to meet the inspector before reaching the land. He was a mere boy who looked at my papers coldly and without comment, except to ask me (prompted by an old fellow who was steering his boat) if I had no paper from the collector at Villa Nova. I told him no, that I was no *commerciante*, had nothing to sell, and that he had read my passports from his government. After a little hesitation he suffered me to pass.

The pull into the right bank had brought me to the head of an island. The inspector told me that the passage was as short on that side, but that it was narrow, and full of *carapana*, as mosqui-

toes are called on the Amazon. Although I have a mosquito curtain which protects me completely, the boatmen have none. Whenever I stop at night, they have a wretched time. This is one of
the reasons why I have been travelling at night.

We pulled back into the main stream, drifted all night, and by
morning reached the country where the cocoa is regularly cultivated. The banks of the river presented a much less desolate and
savage appearance than they did above. The cocoa-trees have a
yellow-colored leaf, and this, together with their regularity of
size, distinguishes them from the surrounding forest. At 8 P.M.,
February 25, we arrived at Obidos, one hundred and five miles
below Villa Nova. Several gentlemen offered to furnish me a
vacant house, but I was surly and slept in my boat.

Whilst at Obidos, I took a canoe to visit the *cacoaes,* or cocoa
plantations, in the neighborhood. The fruit is called *cacao.* We
started at 6 A.M., accompanied by a gentleman named Miguel
Figuero, and stopped at the mouth of the Trombetas which
empties into the Amazon four or five miles above Obidos. The
Trombetas is said to be a very large river, in some places as wide
as the Amazon is here—about two miles.

Near the mouth of this river we stopped at an establishment for
making pots and earthenware generally, belonging to a gentleman named Bentez, who received us with cordiality. This country house was neat, clean, and comfortable. I caught glimpses of
some ladies neatly dressed and with very pretty faces, and was
charmed with the sight of a handsome pair of polished French
leather boots sitting against the wall. This was the strongest
sign of civilization that I had met with, and showed me that I
was beginning to get into communication with the great world
without. Senhor Bentez gave me some eggs of the *enambu,* a bird
of the pheasant or partridge species, some of which are as large
as a turkey.

In crossing the Amazon, we were swept by the current below
the plantation we intended to visit, and thus had a walk of a
mile through the cocoa plantations, with which the whole right

180

bank of the river between Obidos and Alemquer is lined. I do not know a prettier place than one of these plantations. The trees interlock their branches, and, with their large leaves, make a shade impenetrable to any ray of the sun. The earth is perfectly level and covered with a carpeting of dead leaves, and the large golden-colored fruit, hanging from branch and trunk, shine through the green with a most beautiful effect. The only drawback to the pleasure of a walk through them arises from the quantity of mosquitoes, which in some places, and at certain times, are unendurable to one not seasoned to their attacks. I could scarcely keep still long enough to shoot some of the birds that were flitting among the trees and which I wanted for my collection.

This is the time of the harvest and we found the people of every plantation engaged, in the open space before the house, in breaking open the shells of the fruit and spreading the seed to dry in the sun on boards placed for the purpose. They make a pleasant drink for a hot day by pressing out the juice of the gelatinous pulp that envelops the seeds; it is called cacao wine; is a white, rather viscid liquor; has an agreeable, acid taste, and is very refreshing. Fermented and distilled, it will make a powerful spirit. The ashes of the burnt hull of the cacao contains a strong alkali and it is used in all the *cacoaes* for making soap.

We were kindly received by the gentleman whom we went to visit, Senhor José da Silva, whom we found busily engaged in gathering the crop. When he discovered that we had eaten nothing since daylight, he called out in true, hospitable, country fashion, "Wife, cook something for these men, they are hungry," and we accordingly got some dinner of turtle and fowl.

The town of Obidos proper contains only about five hundred inhabitants, but the district is populous, and is said to number about fourteen thousand. There is quite a large church in the town, built of stone and mud, with some pretensions to architecture; but, though only built in 1826, it seems already falling into ruins and requires extensive repairs.

181

There are several shops, apparently well stocked with English and American clothes and French fripperies. I heard a complaint that the trade was monopolized by a few who charged their own prices, but I judged, from the number of shops, that there was quite enough competition to keep the prices down. Senhor Antonio Monteiro Tapajos, a resident of Obidos, was very kind to me during my stay there. He gave me some specimens of Indian pottery, and his wife, a thin, delicate-looking lady, with nine children (the oldest only thirteen years of age), gave me a very pretty hammock.

We left Obidos in the rain the 29th of February. Our long stay at Barra had brought the rains upon us, and we now had rain every day. We travelled all night, and at half-past 9 A.M., on the 1st of March, we reached the town of Santarem. We presented our passports and letters to the Delegado, Senhor Miguel Pinto de Guimaraès, and obtained lodgings in the house of a French Jew of Pará, who was engaged in peddling jewelry.

Santarem, four hundred and sixty miles from the mouth of the Rio Negro, and six hundred and fifty miles from the sea, is the largest town of the province, after Pará. By official returns it numbers four thousand nine hundred and seventy-seven free (eighty-seven being foreigners) and one thousand five hundred and ninety-one slave inhabitants. There are tokens of an increased civilization in a marble monument in the cemetery and a billiard table. The houses are comfortably furnished, though I believe every one still sleeps in a hammock. The rides in the environs are agreeable, the views picturesque, and the horses good. A tolerably good and well-bitted horse may be had for seventy-five dollars. They graze in the streets and outskirts of the town and are fed with Indian corn. There is a church (one of the towers has lately tumbled down) and two or three primary schools. The gentlemen all wear gold watches and take an immoderate quantity of snuff.

I made several pleasant acquaintances in Santarem. One of the most agreeable was a young French engineer and architect, M. Alphonse Maugin De Lincourt, to whom I am indebted for

182

some valuable presents and much interesting conversation. I spent a very agreeable day with him at the country house of another French gentleman, M. Gouzennes, situated about three miles from Santarem. The house is a neat little cottage, built of *pisé*, which is nearly the same thing as the large sun-dried bricks called by the Spaniards *adobe,* though more carefully prepared. I supposed that this house, situated in the midst of a cocoa plantation on low land near the junction of two great rivers, under a tropical sun and with a tropical vegetation, would be an unhealthy residence, but I was assured there was no sickness here. We put up in earth, for transportation to the United States, plants of arrow-root, ginger, manacá, and some flowers.

Other gentlemen were also kind and civil to me. Mr. Bates, a young English entomologist, gave me a box of very beautiful butterflies; Senhor Pinto, the Delegado, furnished me with horses to ride; and I took most of my meals with Capt. Hislop. A young Englishman named Golden, who had married a Brazilian lady and was engaged in traffic on the river, was also kind to me, giving me specimens of India-rubber and cotton.

We had a great deal of heavy rain during our stay at Santarem (generally at night), with sharp lightning and strong squalls of wind from the eastward. The river rose with great rapidity for the last three or four days of my stay. The beach on which I was accustomed to bathe, and which was one hundred yards wide when I arrived, was entirely covered when I left. I left Santarem at 7 P.M., March 28. We gave passage to the French Jew who had provided us with lodgings in his house.

We drifted with the current all night and stopped in the morning at a small cocoa plantation belonging to some one in Santarem. The water of the river was, at this time, nearly up to the door of the house, and the country seemed to be all marsh behind. I never saw a more desolate, sickly-looking place, but a man who was living there with his wife and six children (all strong and healthy-looking) told me they were never sick. This man told me that he could readily support himself and his family but for the military service he was compelled to surrender at Santarem, which took him away from his work and his family for several months in every year.

March 30. We passed this morning the high lands on the left bank of the river, among which is situated the little town of Monte Alegre. This is a village of fifteen hundred inhabitants, who are principally engaged in the cultivation of cocoa, the raising of cattle, and the manufacture of earthen-ware and drinking cups made from gourds, which they varnish and ornament with goldleaf and colors in a neat and pretty style.

In the afternoon we crossed the river, here about four miles wide, and stopped at the village of Prainha. This is a collection of mud huts on a slight green eminence on the left bank of the river, ninety miles below Santarem. The five hundred inhabitants employ themselves in gathering India-rubber and making manteiga, the island opposite the town having a lake in the centre abounding with turtle. Although there were a number of cattle grazing in the streets of Prainha, we could get no fresh meat, and indeed, but for the opportune arrival of a canoe with some fish, our tuyuyus, or great cranes, would have gone supperless.

It is very difficult to get any information from the Indian pilots on the river. When questioned regarding any stream, the common reply is, "It runs a long way up; it has rapids; savages live upon its banks; everything grows there." (*Vai longe, tem caxoieras, tem gentios, tem tudo.*) I am always reminded of the Peruvian Indian with his *hay plantanos, hay yuccas, hay todo.*

The principal trade of this part of the country is in India-rubber, obtained on the Xingu and the neighboring smaller streams. We found everywhere a great demand for salt fish; everybody asked us if we had any to sell. The scarcity of the fish is attributable to the fact that the river has fallen very little this year, but I incline to believe that the fish are not so plentiful and that the people are not so active in taking them as before. It was amusing at Santarem to see the gathering of the population around

184

a canoe, recently arrived with fish, as if this were a thing of rare occurrence.

After we had sailed, the Commandante-militar, to whom I had applied for more men and who had told me there were none to be had, sent a man in a canoe after us. I suspected no great courtesy, and found, accordingly, that the man, a Negro, was a cripple and utterly worthless. He had evidently been palmed off upon us to get rid of him. I made him feed the birds and cook for the men. These men made the best and hardest-working crew I had during my voyage.

About eighty-five miles below Prainha commences the great estuary of the Amazon. The river suddenly flares out into an immense bay, which is probably one hundred and fifty miles across in its widest part. This might appropriately be called the "Bay of the Thousand Islands," for it is cut up into innumerable channels. The great island of Marajó, which contains about ten thousand square miles, occupies nearly the centre of it and divides the river into two great channels—one, the main channel of the Amazon, which runs out by Cayenne, and the other and smaller one, the river of Pará. I imagine that no chart we have gives anything like a correct idea of this bay. The French brig-of-war *Boulonnaise,* some years ago, passed up the main channel from Cayenne to Obidos and down the Pará channel, making a survey ; but she had only time to make a survey of the channels through which she passed, leaving innumerable others unexplored. I think it would cost a steamer a year of uninterrupted labor to make a tolerably correct chart of this estuary.

At this point we turned into a small creek that penetrated the right bank, and ran for days through channels varying from fifty to five hundred yards in width, between innumerable islands. This is the India-rubber country. The shores of the islands were all low. Indeed, we seldom saw the land at all, the trees on the banks generally standing in the water. We stopped at one of the several establishments on the river for making, or rather for buying,

185

India-rubber. The house was built of light poles, and on pilings to keep it out of the water, which, at this time, flowed under and around it. The owner had a shop containing all the necessaries of life and such articles of luxury as were likely to attract the fancy of the Indian gatherers of the rubber. It was strange, and very agreeable, to see flour-barrels marked *Richmond,* and plain and striped cottons from *Lowell* and *Saco,* with English prints, pewter rings, combs, small guitars, cheese, gin, and aguadiente, in this wild and secluded-looking spot.

April 4. The channels and shores are as before, though we occasionally see a patch of ground with a house on it. This is generally surrounded with cocoa-nut trees and other palms, among which the *miriti* is conspicuous for its beauty. This is a very tall, straight, umbrella-like tree that bears large clusters of a small nut, which is eaten.

We arrived at Breves, on the island of Marajó, at 11 A.M. This settlement is about two hundred miles below Gurupá. It is a depot of India-rubber. It has a church, several shops, and seems a busy, thriving place. We employed the 5th, 6th, and 7th of April in running through island passages, and occasionally touching on the main stream, anchoring during the flood-tide. I could keep no account of the tide in these passages. We would encounter two or three different tides in three or four hours. I imagine the reason of this was that some of the passages were channels proper of the Amazon; some of them small, independent rivers; and some, again, *furos,* or other outlets of these same rivers. I could get no information from our pilot. He seems to me to say directly contrary things about it. The old man is very timid and will never trust himself in the stormy waters of the main river if he can find a creek, though it go a long distance about. The channels are so intricate that we find, at the bifurcations, bits of sail cloth hung on the bushes, to guide the navigators on the route to Pará.

April 8. The pilot objected to attempt the passage of the bay, but another pilot, who was waiting to take a vessel across the

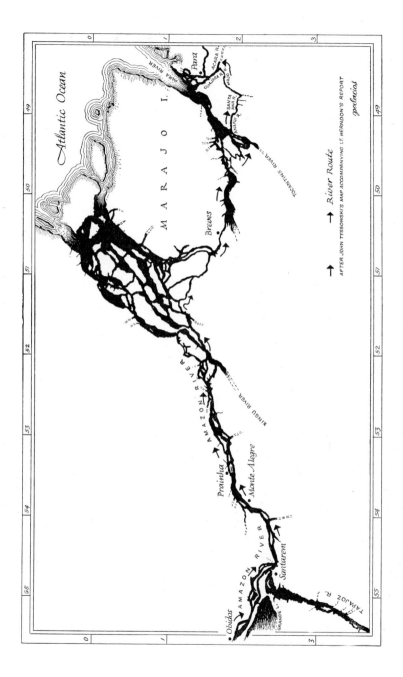

AFTER JOHN TYSSOWSKI'S MAP ACCOMPANYING LT. HERNDON'S REPORT

next day, encouraged him, telling him that he would have *feliz viagem.*

We pulled a mile to windward and made sail across. The wind from the northward and eastward, encountering the ebb-tide which runs from the southward, soon made a sharp sea, which gave us a rough passage. The canoe containing our animals and birds, which was towing astern, with our cripple Negro from Gurupá steering, broke adrift, and I had the utmost difficulty in getting her again; indeed we took in so much water in our efforts to reach her that I thought for a moment that I should have to make sail again, and abandon the menagerie. The canoe, however, would probably not have perished. She was so light that she took in little water, and would have drifted with the ebb-tide to some point of safety.

We had a quick run to an island near the middle of the bay, about five miles from the shore that we sailed from. The bay on this side of the island has several sand-flats that are barely covered at low water. They seem entirely detached from the land and have deep water close around them.

Our pilot must have steered by instinct or the direction of the wind; most of the time he could see no land, so thick and heavy was the rain. He grinned with delight when we ran under the lee of the island and I nodded my head approvingly to him and said, *"Bem feito, piloto* ("Well done, pilot"). We breakfasted on the island and ran with the flood-tide to its southern extremity, when, turning to the north, we had the flood against us, and were compelled to stop.

We crossed the other arm of the bay (about five miles wide) with the ebb-tide, and anchored at the mouth of a small river called Anapui, which empties into the bay near its opening into the main river of Pará.

There are large mud flats near the mouth of this river which are enclosed with small stakes driven in the mud close together, for the purpose of taking fish when the tide is out. A great many small fish, about the size of a herring and called *mapará,* are taken and salted for food. The fishermen, in ludicrously small canoes, gathered around us, admiring our birds and asking many strange questions.

This river is about two hundred and fifty yards wide and has a general depth of thirty-six feet. Its banks are lined with plantations of cane, sugar-mills, and potteries. Nearly all the rum and the pots for putting up the turtle-oil that are used on the river are made in this district. The river empties into the Anapui. We anchored at its mouth to wait for the flood-tide. Our pilot, who always sleeps on the arched covering over the stern of the boat, rolled overboard in the night. The old man swam well, or he would have been lost.

The village of Santa Ana is eight miles from the mouth of the river. It is the centre of the rum and molasses trade of the district. It is a small, neat-looking village of about five hundred inhabitants, and the country around is very thickly settled. Just above the village we entered the mouth of a creek, six miles of navigation on which brought us to a canal which connects with the river Mojú. We found the Mojú a fine stream of about four hundred yards in width. The water was brown and clear, and the banks everywhere three or four feet out of the water. I was surprised to see so few houses on its banks. It looked very nearly as desolate as the Marañon in Peru.

A descent of forty-five miles on the Mojú brought us to the junction of the Acará, which comes in from the southeast. The estuary formed by the junction of the two rivers is about two and a half miles wide and is called the river Guajará. Five miles of descent of the Guajará brought us to its entrance into the Pará river, five miles above the city, where we arrived at half-past 9 P.M. on the 11th of April.

I was so worn out when we arrived, that, although I had not heard from home, and knew that there must be letters here for me, I would not take the trouble to go to the consul's house to seek them. Sending Mr. Potter and the Frenchman ashore to their families, I anchored in the stream, and, wrapping myself in my blanket, went sullenly to sleep.

The charm, however, of Mr. Norris's breakfast table next morning—Mr. Norris being the American consul—with ladies and children seated around it, conversing in English, might have waked the dead. Under the care and kindness of himself and his family, I improved every hour and was soon in condition to see what was to be seen, and learn what was to be learned, of the city of Pará.

CHAPTER XIII

Pará

*   *   *

The city of Santa Maria de Belém do Grão Pará, founded by Francisco Caldeira do Castello Branco in the year 1616, is situated on a low elbow of land at the junction of the river Guamá with the river Pará at a distance of about eighty miles from the sea. Pará is not fortified, either by land or water. There is a very small and inefficient fort situated on an island about five miles below the city, but it is only armed with a few ill-conditioned field-pieces which do not command the channel. There is also a small battery in the city near the point of junction of the two rivers. There are no guns mounted, however, and its garrison could be easily driven out by musketry from the towers of the cathedral.

The harbor is a very fine one. There is an abundance of water and ships of any size may lie within one hundred and fifty yards of the shore. There is a good landing-place for boats and lighters at the custom-house wharf, and at half tide at the stone wharf, some five hundred yards above. The city is divided into the *frequezias,* or parishes, of Sé and Campina. Nine other frequezias are included in the *municipio* of the capital but many of these are leagues distant and should not geographically be considered as belonging to the city, or their population be numbered in connection with it. The population of the city proper numbered, in 1848 (the last statistical account I have, and which I think would differ very little from a census taken at this time), nine thousand

192

two hundred and eighty-four free persons, and four thousand, seven hundred and twenty-six slaves.

Pará was a remarkably healthy place, entirely free from epidemics of any kind, until February, 1850, when the yellow fever was taken there by a vessel from Pernambuco. It was originally brought from the coast of Africa to Bahia and spread thence along the coast. The greatest malignancy of the disease was during the month of April, when it carried off from twenty to twenty-five a day. About the same time the next year (the fever being much diminished), smallpox broke out with great violence. I ascertained that about twenty-five per cent of the population died from the two diseases.

The rich vegetation of the country much enhances the beauty of the city. In nearly all the gardens grow the beautiful miriti palm, the cabbage palm, the cocoa-nut, the cinnamon, the bread-fruit tree, and rich green vines of black pepper. The rapidity of vegetable growth here is wonderful. Streets opened six months ago in the suburbs of the city are now filled up with bushes of the *stramonium,* or Jamestown weed, fully six feet in height. There are a number of almond trees, which are very ornamental, in various parts of the town. These trees throw out horizontal branches, encircling the trunk at intervals of five or six feet, the lowest circle being the largest, so that they resemble in shape a Norfolk pine.

We saw, in a walk in the suburbs of the town, what we thought to be a palm tree growing out of the crotch of a tree of a different species, but upon examination it appeared that the tree out of which the palm seemed growing, was a creeper, which, embracing the palm near the ground, covered its trunk entirely for fifteen or twenty feet and then threw off large branches on each side. It may seem strange to call that a creeper, when it had branches of at least ten inches in diameter, but so it was. It is called the parricide tree, because it invariably kills the tree that supports it. The most picturesque object, however, in Pará was the ruins of an old opera house near the palace. The luxuriant vegetation of the

193

country has seized upon it, and it presents pillar, arch, and cornice of the most vivid and beautiful green.

The society of Pará is also agreeable. The men, I am sorry to say, seem to be above work. Most of them are *hidalgos*, or gentlemen, and nearly all are in the employ of the government with exceedingly small salaries. In the whole city of Pará, I am told, there are not a dozen Brazilians engaged in trade of any kind. The women are simple, frank, and engaging in their manners, and very fond of evening parties and dancing. I attended a ball, which is given monthly by a society of gentlemen, and was much pleased at the good taste exhibited in its management. Full dress was forbidden. No one was permitted to wear diamonds, and the consequence was that all the pretty girls of the merely respectable classes, as well as the rich, were gathered together and had a merry time of it.

But the principal charm of Pará, as of all other tropical places, is the *dolce far niente*. Men, in these countries, are not ambitious. They are not annoyed, as the more masculine people of colder climates are, to see their neighbors going ahead of them. They are contented to live and to enjoy, without labor, the fruits which the earth spontaneously offers.

I saw a number of curious and beautiful animals in Pará. Mr. Norris had some electric eels and a pair of large and beautiful anacondas. I had never heard a serpent hiss before I heard these, and the sound filled me with disgust and dread. The noise was very like the letting off of steam at a distance. The extreme quickness and violence with which they darted from their coil (lacerating their mouths against the wire-work of the cage) was sufficiently trying to a nervous man, and few could help starting back when it occurred. These animals measured about eighteen feet in length, and the skin, which they shed nearly every month, measured eighteen inches in circumference. They seldom ate; a chicken or a rat was given to them when it was convenient. They killed their food by crushing it between their head and a fold of their body and swallowed it with deliberation.

194

Many gentlemen had tigers about their establishments. They were docile and playful in their intercourse with acquaintances, but they were generally kept chained for fear of injury to strangers. Their play, too, was not very gentle, for their claws could scarcely touch without leaving a mark. Mr. Pond, an American, had a pair of black tigers that were the most beautiful animals I have ever seen. The ground color of the body was a very dark maroon, but it was so thickly covered with black spots that, to a casual glance, the animal appeared coal black. The brilliancy of the color, the savage glare of the eye, the formidable appearance of their tusks and claws, and their evidently enormous strength gave them a very imposing appearance.

It remains for me but to express my grateful acknowledgments for personal kindness afforded by many gentlemen of Pará, particularly by Mr. Norris, the consul, and by Henry Bond Dewey, Esq., now acting consul. These gentlemen were unwearied in their courtesy, and to them I owe the information I am enabled to give concerning the history and present condition of the province and the city. On May 12th, by kind invitation of Captain Lee, I embarked for the United States in the surveying brig *Dolphin,* having previously shipped my collections on board of Norris's clipper barque the *Peerless.*

INDEX

199

Shepherd, 28, 33
Shipebos Indians, 120, 122
Silva, José da, 181
Sion, 84
Solimões river, 107, 152

T

Tabatinga, 149–152
Tamitari, 175
Tarapoto, 89–91, 94
Tarma, 9, 32–37, 45
Tarma, Cura of, 33, 36
Taylor, Zachary, 1
Teffé river, 161, 162, 166
Ticumas Indians, 124, 144–147, 158, 160
Tierra Blanca, 121, 123
Tigre Yacu, 108
Tingo Maria, 68, 71–73
Tio Seco, 43
Tocache, 70, 79–81
Tocache river, 83
Tomas, 167
Trinidad, 6
Trombetas river, 180
Tulumayo river, 42
Tunantins river, 154

U

Ucayali river, 8, 49, 65, 109, 112, 128
Ulloa, Antonio de, 7
Urarinas, 108

Urquia, Andres, 128
Ursoa, Pedro de, 6
Utcuyacu, 44

V

Valdivia, Father, 135, 140
Valparaiso, 1, 2
Vega, Garcilasso de la, 3
Villa Nova, 176
Villamil, 70
Viuda pass, 51

W

Williams, Marcus, 162–163, **169, 170**

X

Ximinez, Señor, 19
Xingu river, 184

Y

Yaguas Indians, 135–139
Yahuar Huaccac, 3
Yameos Indians, 125
Yanacoto, 18
Yates, 170
Yavari river, 143, 152
Ytenes river, 8
Yupanqui, 10
Yurimaguas, 97, 102